KARL MARX

THE MAN AND HIS WORK

and

The Constructive Elements of Socialism

Three Lectures and Two Essays

By

KARL DANNENBERG

Price, Thirty Cents

THE RADICAL REVIEW PUBLISHING ASSOCIATION
202 EAST 17th ST., NEW YORK CITY
1918

Reprint from the July-September, October-December, 1917, January-March and April-June, 1918, issues of "The Radical Review"

AT the same time, and quite apart from the general servitude involved in the wages system, the working class ought not to exaggerate to themselves the ultimate working of these every-day struggles. They ought not to forget that they are fighting with effects, but not with the causes of those effects; that they are retarding the downward movement, but not changing its direction, that they are applying palliatives, not curing the malady. They ought, therefore, not to be exclusively absorbed in these unavoidable guerilla fights, incessantly springing up from the ever-ceasing encroachments of capital or changes of the market. They ought to understand that, with all the miseries it imposes upon them, the present system simultaneously engenders the **material conditions** and the **social forms** necessary for an economical reconstruction of society. Instead of the **conservative** motto, **"A fair day's wages for a fair day's work!"** they ought to inscribe on their banner the **revolutionary** watchword, "Abolition of the wages system!"—**Karl Marx.**

CONTENTS

KARL MARX:

THE MAN AND HIS WORK

A STUDY IN HISTORICAL MATERIALISM

FIRST LECTURE

I.

Workingmen and Workingwomen:

THERE is probably no name in the labor movement today, yes and in the scientific world, which is more revered and idolized than that of the founder of scientific Socialism: Karl Marx. In the proletarian movement the name of Marx has become a synonym for scientific soundness and irrefutable accuracy on the one hand, and also a cloak with which to cover and label the most spurious intellectual wares on the other. In scientific circles practically the same conditions prevail, only with the gratifying exception that here the distorters and corrupters of Marx: the Mallocks, Boehm-Bawerks, Skeltons and Simkhovitches, quickly meet their Waterloo at the hands of a competent Marxian, and are thus prevented from accomplishing any further confusion and material harm. As implied above, in the labor movement or Socialist movement proper the task is not so simple, yes a great deal more difficult, and the reason for this peculiarity is to be found in the astonishing ignorance prevalent amongst so-called Marxian Socialists on matters Marxian; furthermore in the fact that the corrupter and distorter of Marx in this case generally carries on his work, knowingly or unknowingly matters little, in the name of Socialist propaganda or under the cover of Marxism.

With so many of his great predecessors, Karl Marx, in the course of years and through the highly scientific character of his works, has been gradually elevated to the position of an infallible demi-god by veritable legions of adherents. Thousands, yes hundreds of thousands of sincere and well meaning Socialists never tire of acclaiming their allegiance to the teachings of this great economist, but—and this is a most regrettable truth—very rarely will the inquisitive seeker find a disciple amongst these masses who has intelligently read or studied the works of his idol. Nothing is more repulsive and disgusting than just this unqualified Marx-deification: a deification which like all idolatry finds its source in the ignorance of the masses, and a deification which is everything but a tribute to Marx and his teachings. To combat just these godlike conceptions of Marx and to familiarize the workers with the social significance of this truly great individual, is one of the cardinal objects of these lectures.

I fully appreciate the largeness of this task, also the impossibility to present to you even a fair pen-picture of the man, or an adequate synopsis of his theoretical system in the limited time at my disposal. These lectures, therefore, do not lay claim to exhaustiveness, neither are they to be considered a condensed compendium or handbook of Marxism made easy. Socialist literature is already plentifully supplied with works of this kind, many of which are excellent, and still more that would have performed a great service to Socialist clarity had they remained unwritten.

My aim in presenting these lectures is to bring the man and social creature Marx nearer to you. I would like to interest many of my comrades and fellow men in the teachings of this master of Socialist letters. To do this successfully, that is correctly, we must examine the historic conditions and the more immediate social atmosphere out of or in which Marx came to be and developed. By becoming familiar with the life of Marx and the distinct material conditions of which this life was but a product, much of the sanctimonious hero-worship will sink into oblivion, and make room for an intelligent appreciation based upon a sound perception. If I succeed in arousing and stimulating the interest of my auditors to the extent that they will make an effort to study and familiarize themselves with the works of Marx, then I believe the purpose of these lectures has been accomplished.

With these few preliminary remarks as a compass before us,

let us embark on our journey into the fields of Marx and Marxism.

It is now practically a half century ago that Marx presented the first volume of his immortal work "Capital" to the world: a work which for the first time, since the inception of the capitalist mode of production, laid bare the laws and forces governing this economic structure. Through the analysis of capitalist production, Marx exposed the source of all profits, and showed this to rest in the appropriation of surplus value from the workers. His theory of surplus value is a most valuable addition to classical political economy, and raises itself upon the theories of value evolved by Petty, Ricardo and Adam Smith, however, also supplemented and perfected by Marx. With the aid of this theory, Marx demonstrated that although the worker under the system of capitalist production receives in the last analysis the full value of his labor-power, he is nevertheless exploited, because he produces in excess of this value, and does not receive the full value of his product.

Going out from the theory of value as evolved by classical political economy of which Ricardo was the last representative, and which formulated that the value of a commodity is determined by the quantity of labor time consumed in its production, Marx started to analyze the only thing the worker has left to sell, namely his labor-power, and also stamped this a commodity. And in just this commodity-status of labor-power he conceived the source of all profit and the source of all accumulated wealth. Marx clearly pointed out that the value of the worker's labor-power is determined by the same law that controls the values of all other commodities, namely: that the value of a worker's labor-power is also fixed by the volume of socially necessary labor time required to produce the commodities necessary to maintain the life of a wage-slave, i. e., that the articles—food, clothes, shelter, etc.,—consumed by the worker in order to sustain life, a life that is again fixed by a certain historical and social standard, determine the size of his wage. Marx now shows that due to its physical peculiarities and the wonderful productivity of our age, labor-power is the only commodity which in the process of productive consumption yields far more than its value, i. e., far more than it needs to reproduce itself. He clearly underscored that where all other commodities when consumed yield but the value contained in them, labor-power yields far in excess of its value, because the worker is the only commodity which produces or yields far more than what is consumed in its production. And he concluded that all work performed by the worker in excess of the work necessary to keep him alive, or to produce the value of his wages, is surplus work, or surplus labor appropriated by the purchaser of the worker's labor-power, the capitalist.

With the aid of this theory of surplus value, he was able to explain the cause and nature of the periodical crisis or panic in capitalist society. He predicted that as capitalism developed, the markets in which to dispose of the surplus wares, or in which to realize the surplus value extracted from the workers at home were bound to become scarcer, and the industrial depressions more frequent. And in the contradiction between the ever increasing social aspects of production and the growing features of individual ownership; in the contradiction that increased productivity on the one hand spells increased laziness on the other; in the contradiction between over-production and underconsumption —a contradiction which so graphically illustrates the economic status of the surplus-value sponging idler and the exploited proletarian respectively; and finally in the contradiction between social creation and individual appropriation, a contradiction which is the dynamo of the class struggle, Marx saw the inevitable collapse of the capitalist system of production. By cementing his economic deductions with his philosophical system of historical development, known as the Materialist Conception of History, he was able to clearly outline and formulate the historical mission of the workers, a mission based upon hard economic conditions and clearly flowing from and truly in accord with the class interests of the proletariat. As stated before, these interests he found were but the logical product of the material conditions underlying capitalist production: conditions which were bound to make the workers conscious of their class interests, and develop to such a climax where the expropriation of the expropriators would become a dictate of historic evolution: where individual social property would give way to social individual property, as the next step in the dialectical process of social development.

Practically fifty years have elapsed since the publication of the first volume of "Capital," and the formulation of the theories just touched upon. And on March 14th of this year it will be thirty-four years since Karl Marx has passed from us. In these days of hurry and scurry, thirty-four years seem a veritable age. How many refutations, corrections, revisions, and annihilations of Marxism were we not compelled to witness in this short span of time? Let me again remind you of the Brentanos, Mallocks, Simkhovitches, Skeltons, Boehm-Bawerks, Bernsteins and consorts. Consider the bulky tomes, highly praised by capitalist journals and professorial fossils, they wrote in their valiant attempt to overthrow the theoretical system of Marx; consider how the combined schools of vulgar-economy have thundered for years against the theoretical premises of this proletarian economist; consider how these henchmen of capital, in the face of irrefutable facts and figures, in the face of undeniable conditions, have sought by intimidation and fraud to ignore, stifle and finally corrupt the economic and philosophical deductions of Marx; consider these events well, and then take an inventory of the results accomplished. You will find that the majority of the "learned" books written to refute Marxism have been relegated into oblivion, or, probably, act as dust absorbers on the shelves of various libraries. Of course, the Mallocks, Skeltons and Boehm-Bawerks are still with us and plying their trade vigorously as ever. Are their theoretical effusions, however, taken as serious as of yore? No, they have neutralized the effect of their theoretical vaporings with the poison of their past idiosyncracies, to use a mild term. Only one opponent named above has had the courage of convictions to admit his errors and that was the strongest opponent of Marxism in Europe, the father of Revisionism —Eduard Bernstein. Bernstein has openly admitted himself mistaken in his deductions on capitalist development; since the outbreak of the war he has repudiated Revisionism and Revisionists, and is today the chief collaborator of Karl Kautsky, the foremost exponent of Marxism in the world. At a whole the bourgeois economists, in their attempt to refute Marx's theory of value and surplus value and the logical deductions flowing therefrom, or in their futile efforts to disprove the Materialist Conception of History have failed, yes, miserably failed.

And how many experiments, "practical" experiments along the lines of sugar-coated reforms, social uplift work and philanthropic saps have not been launched, in order to exterminate by practical demonstration the class hatred (understand class-consciousness) inherent in the Marxian conception of society, and so grandly symbolized by the fighting proletariat conscious of its aim. Have these efforts accomplished their task?; have the class cleavages been bridged over, or the antagonism abolished?; is the identity between Capital and Labor today a reality?; and finally, has the class struggle, this diabolical invention of satan, been substituted by social harmony? Has the spectre of Communism ceased to haunt Europe since the issuing of the Communist Manifesto? When we look upon society today, and compare the gigantic accumulations of wealth in the hands of an ever decreasing number of capitalists on the one hand with the, relatively speaking, dependency and misery of an ever growing proletariat on the other; when we compare the colossal struggles between the robbers and the exploited of today with the comparatively pygmean struggles of the past; and when we compare the social relations between the feudal-capitalist and the enslaved worker of our present oligarchic-capitalism with the relations between capitalist and worker of even fifty years ago, then every unbiased student will admit that the class demarcations are sharper drawn, the interests of the conflicting classes more opposed, and the class-struggle raging with greater vigor today than ever before. And, true to the Marxian conception of capitalism, class-lines will continue to become more distinct and the class struggle correspondingly more intensive, the industrial depressions more frequent and the lot of the worker more unsettled, as the capitalist mode of production reaches ever higher forms in its development. To sum up: today, more lucidly than ever, the economic and philosophical deductions and principles of Marx stand verified and vindicated by the force of past experience and the facts of current events—an intellectual oasis in the desert of vulgar-economy.

And the teachings of the founder of scientific Socialism have not only been verified by the undeniable facts of economic evolution, but also by a corresponding increasing class-consciousness accompanying this inexorable historic process. When Marx went to eternal rest in 1883, already more than the proverbial baker's dozen had declared their allegiance to Socialism: it was the period when hundreds and thousands followed the standard of working-class emancipation—the dawn of modern capitalism, and the embryonic stage in the development of the modern labor movement. Today millions of disinherited all over the globe gather around the banner dedicated to the proletariat by Marx: a banner truly expressive of the demands of economic and social necessity, and symbolizing the ideals and historic mission of the working-class—the destruction of the political class state and the inauguration of the Industrial Republic.

II.

Upon the death of Marx, Frederick Engels wrote amongst others to Wilhelm Liebknecht: "The greatest mind of the second half of our century has ceased to think." He ends his pathetic letter with the following glowing tribute: "Whatever we are, we are through him; and whatever the movement of today is, it is through his theoretical and practical work; without him, we would still be stuck in the mire of confusion."

These words may seem pretentious and illogical, especially when uttered by a Historical Materialist, but when we consider the scientific reputation of their author, they command attention and respect. They seem more so pretentious, when we consider that the nineteenth century was particularly representative of great men. Was this not also the century that produced a Darwin, a man who achieved the same results in the field of biology that immortalized Marx's name in the annals of the social sciences? Just as Marx investigated and laid bare the great motive forces and the social laws which actuate and propel the development of society from a lower to a higher stage, so Darwin uncovered and pointed out the dynamic powers and laws of nature which compel life in its simplest form to develop endless-chain-like into more complicated organisms. However, when critically comparing Marx with Darwin, it seems to me that Engels' praise is just. In my humble opinion, Marx was the stronger and more diversified personality. In Darwin we celebrate the scholar, who searched and accumulated knowledge for the purpose of knowing and presenting his findings. His field was far away from the social conflict, and his findings, comparatively speaking, did not affect the social destiny and the class interests of certain social layers so vitally, as did the application of the evolutionary principle by Marx to History and Political Economy. In Marx we notice a blending of the earnest and searching scientist, who yearns for clearness and truth, with the man of action and deeds—the revolutionist. Darwin confined himself to, or at least was forced to confine himself to the establishment of the laws actuating life, i. e., to that what was and is in nature. After Marx had discovered the iron laws governing social development, after he had laid down these laws in the textbook of the proletariat, "Capital," he then did not rest satisfied with his achievements. Marx studied in order to place his findings into the service of social development: in order to actively

FIRST LECTURE   19

participate in the struggle for the Socialist Commonwealth. He
desired to know, so he could act, and he wanted to be well equipped for the task meted out to him and his class-conscious comrades by the unrelenting course of historic events. To him
philosophical clarity implied philosophical clarity to the workers;
the same as we see all his activity radiating from a class-conscious premise and inaugurated solely for the purpose of
abolishing class-rule. He well appreciated, with the aid of the
Materialist Conception of History, the great role the proletariat
had to play in the advancement of society to a higher stage in
civilization; he knew that social evolution had formulated this
position of the workers in the social struggle, but he also knew
that the workers had first to become conscious of their historic
mission in order to fulfill the same successfully—in order to
desire to perform the same.

Writing on the relation of philosophy to working-class activity in the Deutsch-Französische Jahrbücher (German-French
Annals), he gives the following piece of advice to his erstwhile
friends, the Young-Hegelians: "You can not realize a philosophy
without abolishing it." However, he did not forget what he had
learned from them, and addressing the bourgeoisie says: "You
can not abolish a philosophy without realizing it. Just as philosophy finds in the proletariat its material weapons, so the proletariat finds in philosophy its intellectual weapons. The head of
emancipation is philosophy, its heart is the proletariat. The
philosophy can not be realized without the abolition of the proletariat, and the proletariat can not abolish itself without the
realization of philosophy." If the readers will substitute Socialism for the word philosophy, then the last sentence will read:
Socialism can not be realized without the abolition of the proletariat, and the proletariat can not abolish itself without the realization of Socialism.

Before entering upon an examination of the details in Marx's
life, details which are as interesting as they are plentiful and

which in their totality furnish the sum-total of this turbulent life, let us subject the immediate and also the larger social environment out of which and in which Marx grew and developed to a casual examination. I believe, it is quite essential to have at least a general knowledge of the social and historic background overshadowing and influencing every step in the life of this genius, before you will be able to comprehend and appreciate the detailed phases of his tumultuous career intelligently.

Considering Marx's parentage, Klara Zetkin, a profound Marxian scholar, remarks: "The customary theories fail us, when we propound the question how this great personality, this genial thinker, grew and came to be. The parents of Marx were good and intelligent folks, although in no sense intellectually superior to the average. Neither do the family annals of either mother or father point to any ancestor whose intellectual endowments and characteristics remind us of or are comparable to Marx's."

Wilhelm Liebknecht, who for years shared the hard days of exile with Marx in London, writing on this subject states: "On the 5th of May, 1818, at Treves—the oldest German town— among the monuments of Roman civilization and amid the recent traces of the French Revolution that had cleaned the Rhenish province of medieval rubbish, a son was born in a Jewish family: Karl Marx. Only four years had passed since the province of the Rhine had been occupied by Prussia, and the new masters hastened, in the service of the "Holy Alliance," to replace the Heathenish-French by a Christian-German spirit. The pagan Frenchmen had proclaimed the equal rights of all human beings in the German Rhineland, and had removed from the Jews the curse of a thousand years' persecution and oppression, had made citizens and human beings of them. The Christian-German spirit of the "Holy Alliance" condemned the Heathenish-French spirit of equalization and demanded renovation of the old curse.

"Shortly after the birth of the boy, an edict was issued leaving to all the Jews no other choice but to be baptized or to forego all official position and activity.

"The father of Marx, a prominent Jewish lawyer and notary at the county court, submitted to the unavoidable, and, with his family, adopted the Christian faith.

"Twenty years later, when the boy had grown to be a man, he gave the first reply to this act of violence in his pamphlet on the Hebrew Question. And his whole life was a reply and was the revenge."

"Marx's father," writes Marx's daughter, "was a man of great talent, and thoroughly imbued with the French ideas of the eighteenth century concerning religion, science and art; his mother was descended from Hungarian Jews who had settled in Holland in the seventeenth century. Among his earliest friends and companions were Jenny—later his wife—and Edgar von Westfalen. It was their father—a half Scot—who inspired Marx with his first love for the romantic school; and while his father read Voltaire and Racine to him, Westfalen read Homer and Shakespeare to him. And these remained his favorite authors."

It seems to me that the most desirable potentialities of the Jewish race lived in Marx. We find in him the untiring seeker for truth; the seeker who climbed lonely mountain peaks and strove to wrest from the fiery bush that which humanity has sought and striven for since the daybreak of culture: the knowledge of life. Furthermore, we meet here also the tenacious clinging to convictions, and the joy of faith and devotion to a cause: traits which are all predominant in the Jewish race. Then we find in him the flaming rage against injustice and slavery, and that strong developed brotherly feeling, which, according to a biblical legend, prompted Moses to clench his fist to strike the Egyptian who was maltreating a brother of his race. Nevertheless, all these characteristics do not possess anything typically Jewish or racial, because their uniqueness was not developed in sectarian seclusion, and because they are blended or prompted by a cosmopolitanism utterly foreign to the orthodox sectarian: a cosmopolitanism that tears down the boundaries of creed, color or race, and that expresses itself through the brotherhood of man based on the foundation of economic equality. However, wherever Marx's natural endowments, traits which singularly fitted and are no doubt to a large degree the product of the requirements of the historic hour, may come from matters little, especially when we note that in their manifestations they were always placed into the service of disinterested progress in general and into the cause of that class, ordained to be the vanguard of all progress, in particular—the working-class.

We know that Marx's cradle stood in that part of Germany which had been swept over and thoroughly cleansed of medieval refuse by the liberating and invigorating winds of the French Revolution. And, if we take into consideration that the Rhineland borders closely upon that country, which at the beginning of the fifteenth century was the first to give expression to bourgeois sentiments and interests; a country in which capitalism, still shut up in its feudalic womb, ripened first; a country that in those days produced an Erasmus and a Spinoza—the Netherlands; then it will not surprise you, when I emphasize that the Rhenish Province is today and always has been the most classical seat of capitalism in Germany, ergo, also the most progressive province in Prussia or the German Empire. During Marx's boyhood days, the pulsating throbs of the great French uprising were still felt in the Rhineland, and were graphically visible in the bold stand taken by the bourgeoisie against the powers of reaction— a spirit that remained unbroken and rose to its most magnificent heights in the turbulent days of 1848.

And now we come to a time in which Marx developed and worked to advance his views and ideals: the period of his life, and the period of victorious, advancing capitalism. England had practically achieved the mastery over the markets of the world.

France or at least French capitalism was organizing gigantic accumulations of wealth for exploitation. In the sixties, Marx sees how victorious capitalism invades Austria, Italy, yes even Bohemia. He also is compelled to witness the liberation of the serfs by Alexander II., and thus receives valid indications that capitalism has also commenced to revolutionize the empire of the "little father." He further observes how capitalist production spreads across the ocean, and how the new world also succumbs to the irresistible economic forces making for social progress. Everywhere he sees the advancing forces, the dynamic powers of capitalist production, undermining and destroying the old economic foundations, and setting in their place devices more competent to carry on the process of production. And to be sure, these economic revolutions were bound to be followed by corresponding political upheavals whose aim and object it was to adapt the political institutions to meet the requirements of the new and changed economic conditions. The new capitalist society in the making was no exception to the rule: the nineteenth century may be correctly called a century of political revolutions.

In this manner, historical development presented to or spread before the eyes of Marx incomparable economic and political material: data as important to the searching eye of a student as the compass is to the destination of a ship. This development was internationally so plainly conceivable as the growth of plants in a hot-house, and quite naturally attracted the attention and animated the deeper searching intellects of the world to explain the underlying forces of this gigantic process. However, that Marx was able to penetrate and master this large, manifold and chaotic mass of material, that he was able to crystallize the results of his investigation in a manner as clear as crystal, he owes to the German classical philosophy. This philosophy gave him the scientific equipment, the scientific training, without which his achievements would have been impossible.

When the youthful Marx, imbued with an insatiable desire

for truth, began to question the laws of social evolution, the sun of classical philosophy and art was already setting in Germany. Her splendour and warmth, however, still permeated the intellectual atmosphere of this period. The grand philosophy of Hegel particularly continued to affect, influence and live on in the progressive minds. This philosophy conceived everything existing or in a state of creation, whether in nature or in society, as the outcome of a harmonious, well regulated process of evolution: an evolution which in its continuous flow destroys and creates, and whose final cause can be conceived in the self-assertion or movement of the absolute idea. According to this conception, evolution is stimulated or whipped on through the struggle of contradictions or antitheses: a struggle which usually or finally is bound to end with the coming together or amalgamation of the conflicting elements into a higher unit. Governed by the idea of evolution, Hegel's philosophy did not approach the objects of its investigation as completed and fixed creations, which are the same in life as in death, but in their rich diversity of growth and decline, i. e., in their various expressions or manifestations of life. This system of research was known as the dialectic method. Young Marx felt in Hegel a congenial intellect, whose teachings attracted him with an irresistible power. These teachings have been a determining factor in his development and work. Marx, more so than any other man, accepted the legacy of Hegel: a legacy which he found in the concept of evolution. However, as Engels so pointedly remarks: he placed this conception, standing on its head, upon the feet. He sought for the driving forces of historic life not outside of nature or society, not in the mystical absolute idea of Hegel, but as far as history is concerned, in society itself: in the conditions of production and exchange. In what manner, however, and with the aid of what forces these conditions manifest themselves and compel recognition, i. e., by what forces economic and social development is impelled, also the laws underlying these movements, upon these questions Marx threw light with the aid of the dialectic mode of investigation: a method which he had accepted from Hegel and applied with a sovereign mastery.

III.

After young Marx had graduated with honors from the Trier Gymnasium, he matriculated at the University of Bonn. It was the fondest wish of his father, to see his son also a member of the legal profession—a wish, however, which was not to be realized. In Bonn he spent several terms without pursuing any definite studies, and in 1836 we find Marx at the University of Berlin. Here he was for the first time brought in contact with Hegel's philosophy and some prominent Young-Hegelians like Bruno Bauer, David Strauss, Ludwig Feuerbach, etc., who befriended him. As his interest in these problems and studies grew, his nominal studies or "Brotstudium," as the Germans call the grind for an income, were sadly neglected and removed ever farther from the centre of his work and future plans and aspirations. However, as a dutiful son, he continued these studies, but without any great enthusiasm or success, and for the sole reason of avoiding a conflict with his father and to create a source of income for the future. He was also a passionate lover and bethrothed to Jenny von Westfalen, his slightly senior playmate and the prettiest and most refined damsel in Trier. When we peruse some of the youthful poems of Marx, we can about realize the consuming love which he cherished for his beloved, and also how anxiously he looked forward to their wedding day, and how gladly he would have presented a safe and sunny future as a wedding gift to his Jenny.

However, stronger than every other desire there burned in Marx a yearning for knowledge—a desire to know. With an insatiable thirst he entered upon the study of the various sciences, however, specializing in philosophy and history. He consulted scholarly treatises, contemporary life and closely dissected and questioned scientific systems. Overstudy and also the gruelling inner conflict between the feverish wish for clarity and the inexorable duty endangered his health. The future was also beclouded by a threatening conflict with his father. An early death of Heinrich Marx, however, saved Marx from these ungratifying scenes. The youth remained steadfast in his determination. With tenacious perseverance, he devoted himself to his purposes and aims in life; he battled bravely with the sciences; toiled endlessly and unceasingly to achieve results; and he was rewarded for his untiring efforts, not over night mind you, but after many years of profound and conscientious research. Craving for knowledge and desirous of doing things, Marx, as a disciple of Hegel, delved through history, and particularly the history of his time, in search for the absolute idea: the idea that governs and propels everything in life. He desired to study the manifestations of this force in the intellectual progress of the people, in the form and institutions of social life; he desired to vision direction and aim of its effect clearly, in order to be able to serve evolution conscientiously. However, this process of self-enlightenment netted him at first, outside of a few fruitful doubts, only some starting points to his later conception of history. Only after years he found, instead of the absolute idea, the real driving power behind social development; he found the force that has shaped, determined and influenced ideas in history ever since the day society was organized upon private-property, namely: the class-struggles, which again are unchained and have their origin and aim in the conditions of production and exchange prevailing in a community at a certain historic period.

Before he was able to arrive at above conclusions, before he could formulate his findings into a clear and scientific theory, conditions compelled him to discontinue his studies, and with a dissertation on the "Philosophy of Epicure" he graduated, although not present, from the University of Jena in 1841, receiving the degree of doctor of philosophy. He had hoped and harbored the fond ambition to serve the cause of intellectual freedom, by becoming a lecturer at one of the German universities, but the

dismissal of his friend Bruno Bauer in Bonn showed this anticipation to be a dream: a fata-morgana in a desert of bureaucratic
intolerance. And when we today compare these events with
conditions in our universities and other seats of learning, when
we take the disciplining and the spectacular and unwarranted
dismissal of Scott Nearing from the University of Pennsylvania
as an analogy, we will be compelled to conclude that these institutions are as of yore dominated by class interests of the bourgeoisie and everything else but agencies of free thought and
investigation. Academic liberty always was and is a fetish upon
whose altar high-sounding phrases are sacrificed, but which like
so many of our "inalienable rights" is in reality but one of the
many conventional lies. In the face of these insurmountable
obstacles, Marx decided to become a writer. In 1842, still residing in Bonn, he started to contribute to the "Rheinische Zeitung,"
published in Cologne, and whose editorship he shortly afterwards
assumed. This paper was founded by a circle of class-conscious
capitalists of the Rhineland; it was intended to be the official
organ of the Rhenish bourgeoisie, and as such advocated in a
moderate form such constitutional changes and liberties, as conceived by and were to the benefit of the capitalist class. It sulked
against the so-called god-ordained powers of monarchy, aristo-
cracy and bureaucracy; but as a whole the paper presented a
somewhat lame opposition—but it was at least an opposition to
the forces of reaction so dominant and provokingly brutal in
Prussia before the memorable March days of 1848. Under the
editorial guidance of Marx, this opposition gained in force and
sharpness. He stormed against the censorship and advocated its
abolition, voicing the demand for a free and unfettered press.
As a political writer, he severely criticized the proceedings of the
Rhenish Diet, and we also detect here the first manifestations of
an awakening interest in Marx in economic conditions. He
earnestly grapples with these problems to obtain a clear conception, but also feels here the insufficiency of Hegel's philosophy.
The problem of the lumber thefts and the poverty amongst the

wine-growers on the Mosel furnished Marx with actual material in this connection.   These peasants had been alternately exploited and oppressed by the officials of the god-ordained government and unscrupulous usurers, and found in Marx a warm and fearless attorney.   The struggle in behalf of these impoverished peasants was a thorn in the sides of the government, and only tended to swell the already lengthy list of treasonable offences and undesirable acts committed by this now formidable opponent. Shortly and upon explicit decree of Wilhelm IV. the suppression of the "Rheinische Zeitung" was ordered.   Marx was practically now without any means of support and also, and that depressed him still more, without a field of public activity, and without the least possibility of creating such a field in Germany.   In less than two years, it had forcefully dawned upon Marx that any work which aimed at the liberation of Germany from feudal domination was nigh impossible on German soil.   He, consequently, decided to go to Paris—the center of political life and libertarian aspirations.   Before his departure, he was wedded to Jenny von Westfalen after a courtship of seven years.

The material basis for the support of the family in Paris was to be created by the Deutsch-Französischen Jahrbücher ("German-French Annals"), which Marx contemplated publishing in collaboration with Arnold Ruge.   The "Deutsch-Französischen Jahrbücher" were to be a forum for the free expression and cultivation of radical thought; the periodical was to be a literary gauntlet thrown down to the conservative and sterile elements in Europe; and finally aimed to become a factor in the marshalling, organizing and intellectually clarifying the republican or democratic forces in Germany.   As such, the annals were bound to become a medium for the continuation, development and perfection of Marx's search and studies of the driving forces and laws in social life.   In this connection it may be of interest to cite the following lines of a letter which Ruge addressed to Feuerbach on this subject.   Amongst others Ruge writes: "We intend to publish the "German-French Annals" in a foreign country, and desire to discard entirely the mediocre scholastic junk of the old almanachs with the end in view of uniting ourselves with prominent Frenchmen like Leroux, Proudhon, Louis Blanc, may be Lamartine—Lammendis and Cormenin are probably neither procurable or usable—to such an extent, as to have them directly contribute to the journal (French can be read by everybody) and also to function on the editorial board. The title and prospect we will then issue together, and thus suddenly set up the intellectual alliance of these two nations." The first and last copy of the "German French Annals" appeared in March, 1844, as a double number; it consisted of 236 pages, and contained contributions from Marx, Engels, Ruge, Heine, Bakunin, Herwegh, Feuerbach and several others. A series of causes is responsible for the early failure of this most creditable venture. First the financial resources of the undertaking were insufficient and practically consumed in the publication of the first issue. Secondly, the conditions in Germany were not conducive to the life and development of the periodical. In Germany its circulation was forbidden, and the smuggling of the books over the border was attended with heavy costs and ungratifying difficulties. Neither did the collaboration of the French writers, as anticipated and solicited, materialize. Finally the break and everlasting disagreement of Marx with Ruge was a tributary cause which aided in undermining the young life of the periodical. Marx, who through his historic philosophical conception was daily creating a wider gulf between himself and his associates, was unable to accept or subscribe to the views of Ruge on many important topics, until these differences culminated into an open quarrel that finally led to a severance of connections. These tempestuous days of strife and uncertainty reached their climax, when in 1845 Marx was expelled from Paris by the liberal government of that fossilized citizen-king, Louis Phillipe. Behind this act the untiring efforts of the Prussian government were plainly visible: a government which in this surreptitious manner sought to gratify its base lust for revenge on the hated and much feared revolutionist.

Poor in material possessions but rich in intellectual values, Marx and his young wife were compelled to leave Paris in search of a new exile. In Paris he definitely concluded his discourse with Hegelianism, i. e., with the Hegelian conception that proclaimed the absolute idea as the driving force in historic evolution. The great French Revolution served him as a mine of historic treasures from which he drew lesson after lesson of social significance. And the profound study of this gigantic epoch in the evolution of mankind, so ably laid down in "The Holy Family; or a Critical Critique against Bruno Bauer and his Followers," finally ripened his materialist conception of history. In the manifestations of this period of colossal upheavals, he found the real potential force that set the idea in motion, the force *behind* all ideological activity, and the force which was the generator of this as well as all previous historical dramas, namely: the struggle of classes. And the formulation of this conception also furnished him with an explanation of the passionate and turbulent life in Paris—a life which was but the forerunner of the February revolution. With the aid of the material gathered in Paris, he was able to estimate the value which the elements of production and exchange played in social evolution, and finally concluded that these were the ultimately determining forces, the so-called basic powers, in social development. In his book "The Holy Family," addressing his erstwhile Hegelian comrades on this subject, he scornfully hurls the following expressive questions at them: "Do these gentlemen think that they can understand the first word of history so long as they exclude the relations of man to nature, natural science and industry? Do they believe that they can actually comprehend any epoch without grasping the industry of the period, the immediate method of production in actual life?"

Equipped with this theoretical key, Marx was able to discern, dissect and explain the complicated and confused political atmosphere in France as well as in the other European countries. Everywhere the powerful rays shed by the searchlight of Historical Materialism penetrated the superficial but popular misconceptions of political issues; everywhere they laid open the deeper, underlying laws of social activity; and everywhere they traced the basic force, animating this activity and formulating these issues, to the material conditions in society. And when Marx ascertained the factors governing social activity and found them to rest in the prevailing system of production of a given historic period, then he had also found the answer to the question of the ultimate outcome of the class war: an answer that contained the goal and course for future working-class activity.

It is to Frederick Engels that Marx owes the fruitful suggestions which led to this epoch-making and revolutionary discovery. Engels, filled with libertarian aspirations and in his "Sturm und Drang" phase of life, had come to Paris in 1844. He became acquainted with Marx and quickly attached to him. This acquaintance was to result into a lifelong friendship: a friendship that was to be cemented by many years of literary collaboration and activity in the labor movement, and which furnishes silent testimony to the beautiful devotion with which these master-minds served the cause embodying their principles and ideals—the cause of the disinherited and exploited workers. Engels was also a graduate from the Hegelian school. It was, however, not History which had sharpened and trained his vision to perceive the laws of social development, but the industrial conditions of highly developed capitalist England. Engels was the son of a prominent manufacturer in Barmen, a highly developed industrial city in the Rhenish Province, who entertained quite some business relations with England and had a branch office of his undertaking in Manchester. Actual business practice had given him a thorough insight into the structure and the various phases of capitalism, and upon this solid foundation he based his final conceptions of the role played by the conditions of production and exchange in historical evolution. In conjunction with these practical observations, the fearful effects of the capitalist system in England flashed the importance of private ownership under capitalist production upon his mind, and exposed to him the source of the innumerable contradictions so peculiar to capitalist society. Following these thoughts to their logical conclusion, it was but natural, and also only the consequence of a firmly established historical conception, to conceive of the economic necessity of converting the private ownership in the means of production into communistic property. And in the above rough, imperfect and still vague conclusions and appreciations, we can see the raw material out of which the Materialist Conception of History was constructed, and which together with this theory furnished the basic elements necessary for the establishment of scientific Socialism. It was up to Marx and Engels to clarify, amplify and develop these elementary truths, and this they have masterfully accomplished in the many years of joint efforts. Today the fruit of these efforts can be seen in the classical Socialist philosophy: a philosophy which has withstood the onslaughts of the master-minds of bourgeois intelligence; a philosophy, which furnishes scientific and incontrovertible knowledge appertaining to the cause, goal, driving forces and course of historic life; and a philosophy which is truly the beaconlight of the proletariat in its struggle for emancipation.

The intellectual struggle of these two men for clarity, this slow process full of doubt, speculation and relentless self-criticism, has been productive of brilliant documents. In these days Marx wrote "Zur Kritik der Hegelschen Rechtsphilosophie" (a criticism of Hegel's Philosophy of Law), "Zur Judenfrage" ("The Jewish Question"), being a reply to Bruno Bauer's metaphysical treatment of the subject as visioned by a historical materialist, and "Die Heilige Familie" ("The Holy Family") to which I have already referred in the preceding paragraph, and to which also Engels contributed. From Engels we find "Umrisse zu einer Kritik der Nationalökonomie" ("An Outline to a Critique of Political Economy"), "Die Lage Englands" ("England's Situation"), and later that masterly sociological study "Die Lage der Arbeitenden Klasse in England" ("The Condition of the Working Class in England in 1844").

During his short stay in Paris, Marx also familiarized himself with the various systems and sects of the French Socialists. Particularly in these years of revolutionary unrest, their teachings enjoyed quite some popularity in Paris, especially amongst the workers and the small bourgeois. To Marx, as a student of all social manifestations, these Socialist tendencies were intensely interesting. He had received but meagre and incomplete news of these activities in Germany, and as a conscientious investigator and student, he was averse to forming an opinion or reaching a conclusion until the actual facts were at his disposal and had been examined. His stay in Paris enabled him to receive first hand information, and to study the theoretical and practical aspects of these movements at their original sources. The first product of this diligent work was his sharp criticism of Proudhon's book "La Philosophie de la Misere" ("The Philosophy of Poverty"), published in 1846. This critical work appeared in Brussels in 1847, under the significant title "La Misere de la Philosophie" ("The Poverty of Philosophy"). Aside from the important fact, that this book completely shattered an obsession with which even up to this late day some Socialists and particularly Anarchists are still taken up, namely that abject poverty is the generator of and a prerequisite to revolutionary vitality, it also contained the first comprehensive exposition of Historical Materialism. Here in his quest for knowledge, Marx for the first time came in close contact with Socialist and revolutionary workingmen—an intercourse which was to be of far-reaching importance to his future work.

Driven out of Paris in 1845, Marx turns his steps towards Brussels. Completely disregarding his really precarious material conditions, and in the face of dire poverty, harassed by the police, Marx continues his activities as a serious student and indefatigable fighter. With an enthusiasm that recognized no bounds, he worked amongst the progressive elements in the labor movement of this city, and to the critical analysis of Proudhon's middle-class Utopianism, he adds a scathing refutation of the confused, hazy sentimental German Communism of the Weitling school. His lectures on "Wage-Labor and Capital," held before a Democratic Workingmen's Club, and the speech on "Free Trade"; also the treatise on "Free Trade or Protective Tariff," published in the "Deutschen Brüsseler Zeitung," show the marked and growing interest which Marx begins to manifest for economic problems. We note here the penetrating thoroughness with which he visualizes and dissects capitalist production, in order to intelligently appreciate its historic character, and in order to be able to define and deduce therefrom the position of the proletariat to the miscellaneous questions of the day. Through their untiring activity and distinguished faculties, Marx and Engels quickly became the centre of a brilliant circle of intellectuals in Brussels. This circle was made up of heterogeneous elements, including impatient Democrats and Socialists from the various parts of Germany, amongst them Wilhelm Wolf, to whom Marx later dedicated his masterpiece "Capital," Moses Hess, Robert Weitling, Ferdinand Freiligrath and others. And through his personal agitation and influence, even more so than through his contributions to the "Deutsche Brüsseler Zeitung," Marx shaped and molded the intellectual development of these German, Russian and French exiles and revolutionists, and thus actually prepared and assisted in whipping on the evolution of things in these countries. In the Rhineland, Westphalia, Silesia and other parts of Germany his friends and disciples were openly or secretly carrying on the propaganda, always in the thickest of the fray, and thus their call and agitation very ominously announces the approach of the revolutionary year.

The first victory for Marxist principles—a victory of international magnitude—was scored, when Marx and Engels received an encouraging invitation from England. London had been for years the seat of a society calling itself the League of the Just.

This organization was composed of revolutionary elements of
various shades, and had been originally a conspiratory society
devoted to the Young German idea, an offshoot of Mazzini's
Young Europe agitation. In 1847, when Marx and Engels were
invited to join the league, this organization represented the only
internationally organized expression of the European proletariat.
Its principles were a mixture of French-English Communism
evolved and born with the aid of German philosophy: They were
teachings as mysterious and hazy as the mystery with which their
propagators surrounded themselves. After a thorough discussion
with Joseph Moll, a representative of the League, Marx and
Engels decided to join the organization, and reorganize the movement along lines fully in accord with their principles: the principles of scientific Socialism in the making. These principles of
Marx in 1847, as today, strove and aimed primarily at the political unification of the laboring classes into a compact proletarian
political party, pursuing a definite revolutionary aim, flowing
from a clear and scientific conception of the workers' position in
society. As we have seen, these principles were not the result of
abstract Utopian speculations, evolved as a protest against the
barbaric injustice and inhumanity of bourgeois society, and pro-
claiming to be the only true offspring of pure reason, divine
justice and true humanity, but were rather the product of a
thorough analysis of the capitalist mode of production: an
analysis which exposed the origin of profit or surplus value, and
thereby projected the inevitable collapse of capitalism. Of course,
such principles based upon the bedrock of sound economics were
bound to collide with the Utopianism on the one hand and the
Nihilism on the other of the various intellectuals in the League
of the Just. Marx anticipated this conflict, but was also convinced that the abstract speculative idiosyncracies of a Cabet or
Weitling were no match for the coherent and irrefutable arguments and recommendations contained in the "Communist Manifesto." In November and December Marx and Engels attended
a Congress of the League in London, and the message of Marx,

which he recommended as the theoretical basis and working programme of the organization and which was practically a rough
draft of the famous Manifesto, was received with great enthusiasm.   The secret organization of the League of the Just was
reorganized into a propaganda society calling itself the Communist League.   Marx and Engels were authorized to draw up a
document setting forth the fundamental principles of the League;
and at the beginning of that stormy, revolutionary year of 1848
the most remarkable and epoch-making document in the annals
of history appeared, a document in which the working-class for
the first time since the inception of modern capitalism proclaimed
itself the deadly enemy of bourgeois society: The Communist
Manifesto.

In the "Communist Manifesto" we view the concerted efforts
of Marx and Engels to present to the world a concise and scientific summary of their ideas.   This document can without any
undue exaggeration be called the birth certificate of scientific Socialism, and was destined to become the declaration of industrial
emancipation for the world's workers.   In the "Communist Manifesto" for the first time scientific Socialism speaks to the world,
and proudly it proclaims its distinctive difference when compared
with the childish antics of Utopian Socialism or Democratic Re-
formism.   In a masterly manner and on a grand scale historical
development is here analyzed, and the causes and forces actuating
this process are exposed to the reader.   This also leads to a dissection and scathing criticism of the capitalist order, winding up
with the convincing demonstration that capitalist society bears
within its womb the material germs of Communism;   also that
this society at the same time rears in the working-class the might
necessary to execute the inexorable dictate of historical evolution.   And in order to make the workers conscious of their historic mission, this masterpiece of keen scientific analysis, concise-
ness and literary beauty concludes with that world-renowned
battle-cry: "Proletarians of all countries, unite!"

To quote the words of Klara Zetkin, a celebrated German Marxist: "The Communist Manifesto, aside from its historic and political significance, will remain a conspicuous monument in the literature of the world; as long as thoughts possess a sense and words have a sound."

SECOND LECTURE

I.

Workingmen and Workingwomen:

THE "Communist Manifesto" was now to be considered the theoretical basis upon which all future activity of the League's members had to rest: all subsequent propaganda, acts and the tactics flowing therefrom were to be evolved in accord or along the lines with the axiomatic principles and aims promulgated in this historic document. However, historic conditions soon compelled the various national groups and members to somewhat loosen their connections with the League, which gave rise to a condition of affairs that bordered upon dissolution of the young organization. Through the compelling force of social events, events which finally culminated into the various revolutionary uprisings of 1848, the workers were forced to unite with the bourgeoisie in their respective countries, and battle unitedly for constitutional government and civil liberties. This struggle of the proletariat and capitalist class against feudal prerogatives gave Marx and his followers the opportunity to propagate their principles in the open: to present for the first time in history the workers' position in this revolutionary drama before the public.

The February revolution in Paris, a revolution that deposed Louis Phillipe, the citizen-king, was the signal for a general uprising against despotism in Europe. This insurrection of the industrial capitalists of Paris against the government of the large agrarian interests (bourgeois as well as feudal) was the summons of social evolution to adapt the obsolete political organs in capitalist society to the changed economic conditions: conditions which were retarded in their growth and development by the antiquated, reactionary and abnormal character of the existing political institutions. In Germany, Austria, Hungary and Italy the smoldering fires of revolt also burst into bright flames, eating and devouring the worm-eaten and brittle social and political remnants of past ages. Everywhere the representatives of modern society vigorously fought for political recognition and rights, and everywhere, even in arch-reactionary Prussia, the so-called god-ordained ruling powers were compelled to capitulate before the united onslaughts of the workers and the bourgeoisie.

The powers in Belgium, which had not been affected by the revolutionary wave, sought to insure their tranquillity by inaugurating a most brutal and unwarranted persecution against Marx and his followers. Under the charge of being alien agitators and inflamers to riot, they were subjected to the most infamous indignities by the governmental officials and finally expelled. Marx and comrades were virtually hounded over the boundary line; the former, in the haste of the moment, being compelled to leave his young wife behind, at the tender mercies of the upholders of law and order. These chivalrous authorities, delighted with the opportunity, gratified their lust for "revenge" by craftily and brutally torturing helpless and penniless Jenny Marx.

Marx retraced his steps to Paris, having been honored by the victorious revolutionary government there with an invitation to return to do practical work. After the outbreak of the revolution, the central committee or executive offices of the Communist League had been transferred from London to Brussels. However, through the autocratic expulsion by the police, these connections were broken up and Marx was momentarily entrusted with the management of the League's affairs, being also charged with the authority to organize a new executive body in Paris. However, Marx's stay in Paris was not to be of a long duration.

As stated before, in Prussia the revolutionary wave had swept away the god-ordained, feudal despotism of the Hohenzollerns. Humiliated and trembling, the king of Prussia accepted the generous but foolish gift of his crown out of the blood-stained hands of the barricade-fighters, thereby accepting

a crown which made him king not by the grace of god, as he had
so haughtily contended before the revolution, but by the grace of
the people—a crown that was restored to Friedrich Wilhelm IV.
in return for certain constitutional guarantees, guarantees which
he subsequently as readily annulled as he had conceded them.

Under such turbulent conditions, it was impossible for Marx
to stay in Paris. He, who had been so often accused of treasonable motives and proclaimed as a man without a country, he, the
outcast, was drawn by an irresistible passion, a feverish longing,
to the fatherland. Taking the given historic conditions as a
criterion, he felt and knew that at home was the field upon which
he could and would fight with the greatest and most telling force
for the revolution in Europe. The ship of the German bourgeois
revolution had followed in the wake of the Parisian uprising, and
in this revolution the proletariat for the first time had affirmed
its interests *as a class,* unfolding the banner of the Industrial Republic. And in Germany the bourgeoisie had only shattered the
absolute monarchy with the massive fists of the proletariat. It
was, therefore, easily conceivable, why in the beginning the bourgeoisie watched the rapid progress of the revolution with anxiety,
and saw in this progress more an element of danger than victory.
This growing class-consciousness of the working-class had sent
a cold chill down the spine of the capitalists, and had greatly
dampened the spirit of elation over the immediate victory. However, one thing was certain: If the revolution were to run its full
course in Germany, i. e., if the revolution were to develop into a
full-fledged bourgeois revolution, a revolution that would sweep
away the last vestige of feudal prerogatives, then all the forces
of the bourgeoisie would have to be enlisted in its cause and
whipped on to a determined struggle. It was clear to
Marx that this revolution could only be victorious, if it
downed, together with the brutal forces of reaction, also
the secret fears of the bourgeoisie for the proletariat.
And in this peculiar creation of history, Marx saw the

duty which for the time being would tax the utmost revolutionary energies of the Communists. And that Germany
was destined to be the next field of battle of the Communists, was
to be found in another deduction made from a peculiar combi-
nation of historic facts. It was Marx's contention that if the
achievements of the revolution were not to be eradicated by a
counter-force, if the waves of the revolution were not to break on
the shores of Russian despotism, then, he maintained, it would
be absolutely imperative to concentrate all the revolutionary forces
on the constitutional or republican development of Germany. A
revolutionized Germany—revolutionized in the fullest democratic conception—he deduced, was bound to be the most massive
bulwark of Democracy in Europe. And this deduction was strik-
ingly verified by subsequent events. Not only did Russian despotism subsequently throw down and drown in seas of blood the
heroic struggle of the Hungarians for independence; not only did
300,000 troops of the Russian despot shatter the revolution in
Austria and save the Hapsburg dynasty; but the failure of the
revolution in Germany—the failure to create that bulwark of
Democracy—was bound to very materially affect the Russian
people's struggle for liberty at a later date. During the Russian
Revolution and after, particularly in the stormy years of 1905 to
1906, the German government viewed with open fear this gallant
struggle of a people for constitutionalism, apprehending with
anxiety the effect which a successful conclusion of this uprising
would have upon the German people. It, therefore, sought to aid
Russian despotism in every possible way to crush the revolt. In
the capacity of henchman of the Czar this government, to the
eternal shame of the German people, arrested thousands upon
thousands of the flower of Russian Democracy in Germany;
hounded thousands upon thousands of Russian students from the
high-schools and universities; and, in true Russian fashion,
searched houses and intimidated the people against the much-
hated "reds." And for what purpose? Did the German govern-

ment expel or try these undesirable residents for a breach of the law or some other valid reason? No, the imperial government was paying its debt of 1849 to the "little father"; the imperial government saw in Russian autocracy a citadel of absolutism and a bulwark, not only against political Democracy, but also against the rising tide of Socialism—the spectre of which was truly haunting Europe and particularly Germany. With fiendish glee Junkerdom and its awe-stricken capitalist lackeys surrendered thousands of Russian fugitives, who had deemed themselves safely out of the reach of the bloody monster, to the executioners of the Czar. And this identical government has today the brazen audacity to bewail and indict erstwhile Russian barbarism, calling itself a pillar of culture.

In Paris, Marx and Engels organized a communist club of German workingmen. Herwegh, the genial poet, was at that time attempting to form a battallion of German republicans for the purpose of invading Germany. Marx very emphatically discouraged this adventurous and highly spectacular and purely sentimental movement, and advised the workers to return to Germany individually and unobserved, and to there begin a revolutionary agitation amongst their fellow-workers.

In April we find Marx in Cologne, one of the most important centers of events and the heart of the highly developed and industrialized Rhine district. He had preferred Cologne to Berlin, because the Code Napoleon, a legacy of the Napoleonic era and the French Revolution, insured to him a greater field of activity and more unmolested movement. At least here political trials were not brought before professional judges of the feudal-bureaucratic state, but tried by a jury. As stated before, in the Rhineland the capitalist mode of production had revolutionized conditions more thoroughly than either in the East of Prussia or the southern part of Germany, consequently, the capitalist class was here more progressive and democratic, and more inclined to a vigorous struggle for a constitutional government. The proletariat, reared by such conditions, was, therefore, comparatively large and intensely revolutionary.

Marx was here confronted with the task to put the theories laid down in the "Communist Manifesto" into practice, i. e., to apply the principles of scientific Socialism to concrete historical conditions. And how splendidly he fulfilled this difficult duty of making the workers conscious of their role and duties in this great struggle of the awakening bourgeoisie against Feudalism; how clearly he emphasized the historical necessity of constitutional government to the development of capitalism—a development which was inseparably interwoven with the growth of an independent working-class movement—can be best appreciated through a perusal of his writings of and on this period. In all the leading cities, friends and disciples of Marx and members of the Communist League agitated and worked along the lines dictated by the "Communist Manifesto." The turbulent times with their various political issues, wage struggles and strikes were thus skilfully exploited and utilized to bring home the message of Socialism and independent class action to the workers. Everywhere clubs and organizations of workingmen sprang up. After the memorable March days, a Central Committee of Workingmen with the Communist Born at the head was organized in Berlin. Through the untiring efforts of this committee, the Brotherhood of Workingmen, an organization that was to embrace and unite all the workers in Germany, was organized in August. Everywhere the workers were seen fighting in the front ranks against the powers of absolutism; everywhere they solidly stood their ground, bravely repulsing the onslaughts of reaction; and wherever they battled most courageously and were nigh unconquerable the communist influence was most markedly recognizable.

This epoch-making phase in the development of Germany is pre-eminently the work of Marx: it is an achievement that was made possible through the intelligence shed by the rays of Historical Materialism—a philosophy which for the first time in

history explained to the disinherited class its place and function
in particularly the bourgeois revolution and society in general.
In the "Neue Rheinische Zeitung" ("New Rhenish Gazette"), a
daily newspaper, Marx sought to erect a beaconlight of the extreme democratic and communist wing of the revolution. The
first number of this paper was published on June 1st, 1848, and
the last issue appeared on May 19th, 1849. The short but stormy
life of the paper, therefore, begins and ends with the fortune and
misfortune of the revolution respectively. The paper was founded
as an "Organ of Democracy"; however, under the editorship of
Marx, it soon became an undaunted and fearless advocate of
communist theories, viewing and criticising current events from
the basic premises as formulated in the "Communist Manifesto"
and conceived with the aid of Historical Materialism. Here the
Materialist Conception of History was submitted to the acid test
and, needless to state, the theory's application to current occur-
rences and the results obtained thereby furnished convincing evi-
dence of its soundness. By the light of Historical Materialism,
Marx explained the revolution as a normal and legitimate historical process, a process which was but the political reflex of an
economic revolution that had but shortly preceded it. Marx,
again with the aid of the Materialist Conception of History, was
able to combine his passionate revolutionary temperament with
a cool and well-balanced historical intellect: he appreciated and
judged the present by the past, and was thus able to intelligently
vision the future.

Marx was a journalist and editor in the broader conception of
the term, and in this connection he was ably assisted by Frederick
Engels, the two Wolffs, Ferdinand Freiligrath, the genial poet,
and others. Equipped with a clear insight and creative revolutionary vitality, the "Neue Rheinische Zeitung" was able to show
the way to the democratic and Socialist forces. And the "Neue
Rheinische Zeitung" was a fighting organ, that engaged and
grappled actively with the problems of the day. As emphasized

before, these problems, and the historical conditions of which they were born, compelled the Socialists and workers to fight as the extreme radical wing in the army of Democracy. The prize of victory and object of the struggle were to save the revolution, and thereby to insure the political rights and liberties necessary to the proletariat for the preparation of its own revolution—a revolution which Marx perceived germinating in the womb of the same society that he and his class were assisting in its struggle to emancipate itself completely from the yoke of Feudalism. For these reasons the "Neue Rheinische Zeitung" was compelled to engage in democratic politics; it was compelled to fight with and for the bourgeoisie, but it discharged itself of this duty creditably, by steadily keeping the ultimate goal and things of permanent interest to the proletariat in view. In other words, the bourgeois revolution was but a means to the end, a stepping stone, to Marx and his followers; the end, the aim to be kept in mind, was—the proletarian revolution. In consequence, the "Neue Rheinische Zeitung" did not seek to enlist the support of the luke-warm democrats with the aid of compromise and flattery, but attempted to whip them on and wrest them out of their lethargy, through a biting and unmerciful criticism. To this organ, as stated before, the revolution was an imperious command of the hour; a command which the bourgeoisie could not ignore but had to follow: a command clearly formulated by the force of material conditions and the scientific knowledge of social development flowing therefrom.

The immediate demands of the Communist Party in Germany were, due to the above-mentioned causes, therefore, far more moderate than the so-called minimum demands formulated in the "Communist Manifesto" for the rising revolution. They were demands chiefly created by the backward conditions of the economic life in that country, and were intended to improve the social conditions of the small farmer, artisan and laborer in general. The cardinal political demands were the undivided republic and the creation of a citizen's army. As pointed out, to Marx the republic in her most developed form was the logical battleground for the settling of the differences between the capitalist class and the proletariat. He further conceived, that the struggle of the Socialists and workers would only begin in earnest, when the struggle for political enfranchisement or Democracy had ended. In the arming of the people, the citizen's army, Marx saw the victory of the revolution. To him constitutional questions were not primarily questions of right but questions of might. And time and time again the "Neue Rheinische Zeitung" underscored that the best constitution was only a scrap of paper, if not supported or backed up by the armed might of the people. And the paper emphasized that all the nicely worded paragraphs and promising clauses in the constitution would not prevent the assassination of the people's rights, as long as the feudalic governments were able to "train their cannons on the untrained people." With bitter sarcasm the "Neue Rheinische Zeitung," therefore, criticised and chastised the garrulous politicians in the National Assembly at Frankfort, who were celebrating rhetorical orgies and entirely neglected to provide the might with which to enforce their legislative decisions. While these political clowns were philosophizing and taxing the people's patience to the utmost, the governments in Berlin and Vienna were in the meantime preparing to mow down the imperial constitution, the freedom of the press and assembly, universal suffrage, and all the gains and achievements of the revolutionary March days, together with its most energetic defenders, with volleys of grape-shot. The criticisms of the German and Prussian parliaments in Frankfort and Berlin respectively belong to the most brilliant publications of the "Neue Rheinische Zeitung." Here we recognize the superior creative power of Historical Materialism asserting itself on the field of politics; and to those narrow-minded dullards, who still think that history is made in parliaments, these angry and passionate, but nevertheless profound critical essays are even at this late date of inestimable value. This critical work of the paper is an important part of a thorough discussion having for its basic theme the principles and programs of the liberals and democrats, and here Marx once and for all and unrelentlessly settles his account with the bourgeoisie. The bourgeoisie acknowledged receipt of this thorough spanking in its own peculiar way: the "liberty loving" democratic stockholders in the paper withdrawing their support from the enterprise. Thereby, however, the paper gained a firmer foothold amongst the workers.

As previously emphasized, the "Neue Rheinische Zeitung" as a beaconlight of Democracy was naturally a most consequent opponent of Feudalism. In no paper was Feudalism or feudal prerogatives fought with more vigor and intelligence than in Marx's paper. Knowing and fully appreciating the importance of the bourgeois revolution, through a thorough conception of Feudalism, Marx and his followers saw in the complete vanquishment of Feudalism a quicker and more favorable development of Capitalism, which in turn implied a quicker and more favorable development of a class-conscious Socialist movement. Therefore, Feudalism and absolutism did not have a more bitter enemy than the "Neue Rheinische Zeitung." And when the counter-revolution, the reaction, swept over Germany; when the treasonable and cowardly action of the terror-stricken bourgeoisie was everywhere perceivable; when Vienna had fallen and the troops of the king were butchering citizens in the streets of Berlin, even then Marx defied the victorious forces of reaction in his paper. And only after the insurrections had been put down in Elberfeld and Dresden, and the Rhineland had been practically turned into a veritable garrison, did the government undertake to suppress the "Neue Rheinische Zeitung." On May 18th, 1849, Marx received his order of expulsion from Germany. Certain editors of the paper were already being persecuted by the courts, and still others were, as undesirable "foreigners," sure to share Marx's fate.

Therefore, the expulsion of Marx was practically the death sentence of the paper. On May 19th the last number appeared with Freiligrath's defiant poem as a leader:

Farewell of the "Neue Rheinische Zeitung"

May 19th, 1849.

No open blow in an open fight,
But with quips and with quirks they arraign me,
By creeping treachery's secret blight
The Western Calmucks have slain me.
The fatal shaft in the dark did fly;
I was struck by an ambushed knave;
And here in the pride of my strength I lie,
Like a corpse of a rebel brave!

With a deathless scorn in my dying breath,
In my hand the sword still cherished;
"Rebellion" still for my shout of death,
In my manhood untainted, I perished.
Oh! gladly, full gladly, the Pruss and the Czar
The grass from my grave would clear;
But Germany sends me, with Hungary far,
Three salvoes to honor my bier.

And the tattered poor man takes his stand,
On my head the cold sods heaving;
He casts them down with a diligent hand,
Where the glory of toil is cleaving.
And a garland of flowers and May he brought
On my burning wounds to cast;
His wife and his daughters the wreath had wrought
When the work of the day was past.

Farewell! farewell! thou turbulent life!
Farewell to ye! armies engaging!
Farewell! cloud canopied fields of strife,
Where the greatness of war is raging!
Farewell! but not forever farewell!
They can *not* kill the spirit, my brother!
In thunder I'll rise on the field where I fell,
More boldly to fight out another.

When the last of crowns like glass shall break,
On the scene our sorrows have haunted,
And the People the last dread "guilty" shall speak,
On your side ye shall find me undaunted.
On Rhine, or on Danube, in word and deed,
Ye shall witness, true to his vow,
On the wrecks of thrones, in the midst of the freed,
The rebel who greets you now!

II.

The "Neue Rheinische Zeitung" had been a piece of political revolutionary practice. The "Neue Rheinische Zeitung," however, was Karl Marx. To speak somewhat with Engels: the editorial policy or course of the paper was "the dictatorship of Marx."

Marx's revolutionary activity in this tumultuous period, however, did not confine itself solely to literary or editorial work. He was also chairman of one of the three large democratic organizations in Cologne. And when we compare the courageous and unified stand of the Rhenish Democracy against the threatening onslaughts of reaction with the irresolute and in many cases cowardly manifestations of the bourgeoisie in other localities, then we begin to perceive not only the effects of a higher industrial and social development, but also the effects of the propaganda resulting therefrom—Marx's propaganda. To illustrate: In Cologne a gigantic mass meeting declared itself for the Socialist Republic, and when a false report was received that the military forces of the reactionary government were advancing to take possession of the city, barricades seemed to shoot like mushrooms out of the earth. In contradistinction to the loud-mouthed but cowardly bourgeoisie of Berlin, the Rhenish and Westphalian Democracy in the eventful November days was willing to support any opposition of the Prussian National Assembly with the utmost development of strength. And when this parliament called upon the people to answer the infamous usurpations of the so-called "god-ordained" autocracy with the refusal to pay taxes, i. e., with an economic strike of the bourgeoisie against the feudal polity, the provincial committee in Cologne, constituted out of Marx, Schapper and Becker, issued an order requesting all democratic unions to adhere to the decision of parliament. The committee, furthermore, instructed the citizens to resist the forceful collection of taxes with all means of opposition at their disposal; to organize the citizen's army everywhere; to supply those without means with arms and ammunition out of the communal funds or with the aid of voluntary contributions; to, if necessary, appoint committees of safety, in order to be effectively prepared to meet force with force. The subsequent despicable and cowardly conduct of the Prussian National Assembly broke this magnificent revolutionary spirit in the bud. However, Marx, Schapper and Becker were indicted before the grand-jury in Cologne on the charge of having incited the citizens to armed resistance against the civil officials and the army. Of greater importance than their acquittal was Marx's masterful speech of defense.

After a year of unceasing struggle, Marx was finally convinced by the inexorable facts of history that the revolution was for the time being at an end; that the bourgeoisie had obtained in the form of social and political reforms all it desired and was

able to obtain with its limited vitality; and that the bourgeoisie—
the same bourgeoisie which had been until a few days ago fighting shoulder to shoulder with the workers against the junkers
and their lackeys—would seek henceforth to ally itself with the
remnants of feudality against the workers. The bourgeois class-
interests dictated such an alliance with the limited feudal government, an alliance which was bound to end with the peaceful
conquest of the government by the bourgeoisie and the permea-
tion of the remaining remnants of feudalism with the principles
and ideas of capitalist production. As an eye-opener, pathfinder
and pioneer, the revolution had brought to the capitalists all they
were able to demand under the existing conditions, always taking
the fear-inspiring Communist workingmen as an ominous sign-
post into consideration. What the force of arms was unable to
accomplish in the stormy year of 1848-49, without also endanger-
ing the existence of capitalist society, economic evolution and its
social and political creatures were bound to realize slowly step by
step. Marx clearly foresaw these logical effects of an abortive
revolution, and also saw therein a dictate to revise the tactics
of the Communists. He fully appreciated that henceforth the
workers would have to organize as a class; that the capitalist
class would, as indicated before, quickly overshadow and absorb
all other minor ruling classes in Germany, including the junkers;
and that, therefore, in the future no pact or compromise with the
"democratically inclined" bourgeois elements would be advisable.
In the middle of April, 1849, Marx and his Communist friends
laid down their offices in the provincial committee. The Workingmen's Club of Cologne severed its connection with the Democratic Union of the Rhineland, and advocated participation of all
radical organizations in a general congress of workingmen which
the Brotherhood of Workers, organized by the Communist Born
in Berlin, was organizing.

With the publication of Marx's "Wage-Labor and Capital,"
the "Neue Rheinische Zeitung" gave expression to these new

tactics. In this keen analysis of capitalist production, the class
distinctions between the proletariat and the bourgeoisie were
heavily underscored, and thereby removed out of the shadow into
which the great historical epoch, the revolution, had for the,
moment placed them.

Exiled from his fatherland, Marx returned to Paris, where
turbulent events seemed to be in the making. Here the capitalist
class, living in constant fear of the proletariat, was preparing its
coup d'état. Of course, to the intriguing and conspiring government of Louis Napoleon this clear-headed, discerning and uncompromising revolutionist was a most unwelcome visitor. Therefore, as early as July, Marx was exiled, this time by a bourgeois
republic, to take up residence in the Department Morbihan, which
is situated somewhere in an obscure corner of the Bretagne. Here
Marx would have been condemned to political as well as scholarly
inactivity—a thing which Louis Napoleon sought to accomplish
by this move. Instead Marx, stripped of all means of subsistence
and with no future prospects anywhere in sight, decided to go to
London. He was certain that the revolution was only temporarily
suppressed, that it was bound to rise again; and he, a stranded
outcast with a family dependent upon him, started to work with
renewed vigor to make the coming revolution a class-conscious
proletarian revolution, as far as the material conditions of that
period permitted and made such a distinct class movement possible. His first task was the reorganization of the Communist
League whose leading men were now practically all in London,
but whose activity was henceforth mainly confined to Germany.
In the "Neue Rheinische Revue" ("New Rhenish Review"), he
sought to provide a fighting organ for the revolutionary forces in
Germany. The "Neue Rheinische Revue" was published in
Hamburg, and, of course, in close collaboration with Frederick
Engels and other friends. Marx desired this periodical to be a
continuation of the "Neue Rheinische Zeitung," and quite posi-
tively hoped to turn this unpretentious monthly into a semi-

monthly and then into a weekly on a large scale. And with a fresh outbreak of the revolution, which he anticipated would be the logical product of the reaction ruling with an iron hand in Germany, the review was to be turned into a powerful daily newspaper. As stated in the foregoing, however, Marx's plans were not to materialize. The tidal wave of the revolution, which had carried the "Neue Rheinische Zeitung," was gradually breaking upon the rocks of a luke-warm bourgeois liberalism. The fears of the capitalist class for the thorough measures and class-aspirations of the proletariat were quickly turning their course into the less dangerous avenue of a parliamentary struggle against feudal prerogatives, a struggle in which the workers as a class were destined to play a historical role, but which forever separated them from the contaminating influence of bourgeois liberalism. But four numbers of the "Neue Rheinische Revue" were published and those under the most ungratifying pecuniary difficulties. Three copies appeared somewhat regularly up to April, 1850, and then after a lapse of four months, the review with a double-number had to definitely suspend publication.

In this periodical Marx and Engels labored to prepare the ground for the anticipated approaching revolution. By subjecting the struggles of the preceding years, struggles in which they had so actively participated, to a critical examination, they sought to accomplish this task. Truly in accord with their Historical Materialistic Philosophy, they attempted to find the connecting causes of these historical and social manifestations and upheavals in the existing class antagonisms, thereby stripping these events of their ideological cloak and exposing the class war in all its nakedness. Aside from distinctly German and in the broader aspect local subjects, Engels wrote a treatise on the Peasant War, and Marx contributed his masterly work, so well known to all Marxian students, "The Class-Struggles in France 1848-1850." This study found its continuation in the profound and brilliant essay entitled "The Eighteenth Brumaire of Louis Napoleon," published in 1852, and its completion in the Manifesto or Address of the Executive Committee of the International Workingmen's Association on the Paris Commune, and better known under the title of "The Civil War in France."

However, the rejuvenated revolution which Marx and his associates so confidently looked forward to, was, as stated before, not to materialize. Subsequent economic and historical studies now showed Marx that the revolutionary year of 1848 had been but the legitimate child of the terrific industrial panic of 1847. And as prosperity gradually surged in upon the troubled sea of European social and political conditions, the revolutionary vitality born by industrial depression ebbed out. An economic era of expansion and plenty had set in, more so intensified by the discovery of gold in California. The anticipation of a rich harvest of profits exterminated the last spark of rebellion in the bourgeoisie. As already dwelled upon above, henceforth the capitalist class was to be guided by only one precept in its political conduct, namely: to harmonize and compromise with feudality and absolutism, in order to jointly exploit the proletariat. The proletariat, however, was as yet weak in numbers, or, to be more exact, weak in organization, and practically entirely lacking in the conscious perception of its historic mission as a class. The collapse of Chartism in England, the June massacre in Paris, the fall of Vienna, the results of the revolutions and struggles in Germany, Hungary and Italy had so physically and morally weakened the workers that for the moment no revolutionary action was to be expected of them. However, the interminable circle of capitalist production, the anarchical features of this production, already foreshadowed the advance of another economic crisis: a crisis that was but the natural child of an economic system based upon the appropriation of surplus-value, and a crisis which in its multiplied form actually portended the inevitable downfall of the capitalist system and the expropriation of the expropriators. These facts Marx conceived with the as yet relatively limited knowledge at his disposal. He also was aware that the workers were only powerful against the exploiters when organized upon class lines—a form and spirit of organization which presupposed class-consciousness. In order to awaken and generate this class-consciousness in the international proletariat, the individual worker had first to recognize his economic status, i. e., to conceive that he was but a commodity under capitalism. Animated, yes whipped on by the compelling command of the hour, Marx set to work to provide the intellectual weapons for the working class in its struggle for emancipation.

III.

Buried amongst the dusty tomes and intellectual treasures of the British Museum, years passed in which Marx once more devoted himself exclusively to investigation and study. They were years of intellectual joys but material privations to Marx and his family. The press as well as the publishers in Germany had instituted a tentative boycott against Marx, and this meant bitter poverty to him and his beloved ones. For example, his brilliant essay "The Eighteenth Brumaire of Louis Napoleon" had to be published in New York in a periodical issued by his friend Weydemeyer. Also the brochure dealing with the trial of some of Marx's comrades before the jury in Cologne and entitled "Enthüllungen über den Kölner Kommunistenprozess" ("Revelations on the Communists' Trial in Cologne") had to be published in America, 1852. During this year, Marx also accepted an offer of the "New York Tribune" to act as its London correspondent; he was expected to contribute an article every week, for which he received the flat rate of five dollars. This meagre but welcome income was practically for years the only regular source of revenue of the Marx family. In the "New York Tribune" Marx published various reviews and criticisms of social and political conditions in Europe, and also a series of articles which afterwards appeared in pamphlet form under the name of "Revolution and Counter-Revolution in Germany." This series of articles was up to a few years ago credited to Marx; the publication of the correspondence between Marx and Engels, however, shows without a doubt that they were written by Engels. "Revolution and Counter-Revolution in Germany" is but a continuation of the historical work commenced in "The Rhenish Review," and its purpose was to show the inner connection, or as Buckle is so fond of saying, "the logical connection," i. e., the historical mechanism of the struggles in the first half of the nineteenth century.

As you will recollect, in his studies, Marx had gone from philosophy to history, and from history to political economy. It is, therefore, quite logical to deduce that a close study of the political class struggles, which since the seventeenth century had swept furiously over Europe as revolutions, brought him in contact with the power or driving forces *behind* and responsible for these upheavals. According to the Historical Materialism of Marx and Engels, in order to intelligently explain the social and political life of capitalist society, the economy or industrial structure of that society must be first investigated and its origin, motive forces, laws and course of development explained. To this task Marx devoted himself during the years of his exile in London, an exile which lasted until his death, with an industry, enthusiasm and disinterestedness truly unparalleled in the history of modern science. As Klara Zetkin so symbolically states: "He devoted himself to this task with the bee-like industry and the patience of the scientist and the revolutionary fervour of the Socialist." The first fruits of his labor were contained in his "Zur Kritik der politischen Oekonomie" ("Contribution to the Critique of Political Economy"), published in 1859, a book which was but a preliminary study of or an introduction to his greatest work "Das Kapital" ("Capital").

The first volume of "Capital" appeared in 1867. It would be the height of folly to even attempt to give a somewhat compre-

hensive review of this monumental work in these lectures. I will,
however, as a conclusion of this lecture, attempt to present to you
a rough but in no form exhaustive resumé of this masterwork,
embracing the fundamental or quintessential principles upon
which the theoretical structure of "Capital" is predicated, and
which to-day are acclaimed as axiomatic truths of the Socialist
philosophy. A knowledge of these philosophical and economic
principles is absolutely indispensable and imperative to an intelligent understanding and appreciation of "Capital," and certainly a
substantial aid in the study of the work. In the last half of my
next and last lecture, I will endeavor to present to you an outline
of a reading and study course for the works of Marx, and let
me emphasize here that a methodical and well-directed study of
writings about and by Marx is also essential for a proper comprehension of "Capital."

To recapitulate part of my first lecture, in "Capital" Marx, in
his search for the basic and causal conditions underlying the
production and exchange of wealth in capitalist society, continued the labors started by the classics of bourgeois political
economy, of whom Wm. Petty, Adam Smith and Ricardo are
distinguished representatives, by dissecting the prevailing mode
of production into its most elementary parts. He found that private property in the means of production is the cornerstone and
historic peculiarity of capitalist society. With the aid of the
Materialist Conception of History, he analyzed the social and
historical position of the proletariat in society, and was able to
formulate the principles and tactics for this class in its struggle
against the bourgeoisie. By fixing the status of the worker in
present society and also exposing the surplus-value creating
faculties of his labor-power; by classifying the worker as a commodity—a living commodity that produces more than it consumes
—Marx laid bare the source and magnitude of capitalist exploitation, and the social and historical function and significance of
capital. By thus uncovering the origin of capitalist society and

defining the nature of its economic laws; by pointing out and
underscoring the transitoriness of and the ever changing forms in
the structure of the mode of production, and the inevitable consequences of competition and surplus-value appropriation, he
entered an indictment of fact against capitalist society and proclaimed the ultimate collapse of this most "perfect" of all systems. Marx significantly and with the aid of his dialectical
method, a method which you will recollect he had taken over from
Hegel, pointed out that a system which originally started with
private individual property had rapidly developed into a system
of private social property, and was bound—through the dynamic
force of class-antagonisms—to culminate into a system of collec-
tive social property. In other words, he was forced to conclude that
the social character of production was bound to be supplemented
by a social system of distribution, and this change was only possible through the abolition of the cornerstone and bedrock of
capitalist exploitation—private property in the means of production. The negation or antithesis of private property Marx found
in social property or—Socialism; and the negation or contradiction of the class struggle he located in the abolition of all classes
and class prerogatives based on any form of property. To illustrate these philosophical deductions: Just as day implies the approach of night, and life portends death; just as truth is born
by the lie, and virtue is but the creature of sin; just as morality is
measured with the yardstick of immorality, and the law is but
the product of an unlawful act; just as the city or town foreshadowed the province, and the province the nation; so the nation
implies the inter-nation; capitalism finds its contradiction in So-
calism; and private property, in its growing social aspects, must
culminate into social property: thus ending the class struggle with
the inauguration of a social peace based on economic equality.
In the past the class struggle found its culmination in the victory
and supremacy of various economic classes, however, these
classes were always swept into power by virtue of certain economic might and holdings, and always asserted their victory to the

detriment of a subject class. The victory of the proletariat is the first victory in which the vanquished class will at the same time become part of the victor class, because this victory is the last phase of the class struggle and announces the victory of society over class rule. Different from all previous struggles in the evolution of mankind, the battle of the proletariat is *not* a battle for proletarian supremacy over capitalist supremacy—a supremacy which is to be asserted at the expense and subjugation of another economic class; the victory of the proletariat does not imply the rule of the proletariat over a subject class, because the victory of the proletariat implies the emancipation of the lowest class in society, the abolition of all property prerogatives, and spells the victory, *not of a class,* but of society.

With "Capital" Marx rendered an analysis of capitalist production unequalled in profundity and thoroughness by any previous or subsequent economist. To the true scientist "Capital" very quickly came to be considered a treasure island of political economy; and to the working class it was and is to this day the intellectual compass, with which the capitalist mode of production through its unique exponent, Karl Marx, has equipped the proletariat in its fight for the liberation of society from class rule.

THIRD LECTURE

Workingmen and Workingwomen:

THE beginning of the last half of the nineteenth century wit-
nessed in the principal European countries and also the
United States an unparalleled growth and development in the
capitalist system of production. It was the period in which the
gigantic cotton industry in the North of England was unable to
procure enough human flesh for absorption and transmutation into
surplus value; it was the period in which the northern part of the
Western Hemisphere was ravaged by a gigantic civil war, waged
to decide the question whether the semi-feudal Southern aris-
tocracy or the, comparatively speaking, progressive and impatient
capitalist class of the industrial North should henceforth dictate
the political policy and economic and social course of the Union;
it was the period in which the gradually awakening Muscovite
Empire, through the at least nominal emancipation of the serfs,
created its first large armies of modern industrial and agrarian
proletarians, and thereby proclaimed to the world the definite
collapse of feudalism and the ascendancy of capitalism in Russia;
it was the period in which the question of political and economic
unity was becoming an ever greater problem and necessity to the
general progress of the German States, and also the crying demand of the hour in torn and disunited Italy; in other words:
it was the period in which the national units of capitalist production became conscious of their interests, and also began to look
with envy upon the colonial possessions and the consequent
imperialistic domination of England; it was the beginning of the
great battle of capitalist national units for international supremacy—a struggle whose culmination is vividly illustrated by the
present Great War. In the sixties and seventies of the last century, of course, the indications for a large era of imperialism
were as yet only mildly perceivable. As stated before, countries
like Germany, the United States and France were still occupied

with the development, organization and exploitation of their national resources or the reformation of their political institutions, in other words: the modern capitalist mode of production was still in its infancy—in its embryonic state.

However, one historic fact loomed forth portentously in all these countries, namely: that in proportion as the capitalist mode of production slowly cast off its swaddling clothes and grew into a vigorous specimen, so the class-consciousness of the exploited masses showed signs of awakening and development. Indications of a growing unrest amongst the workers were visible everywhere. In England the remnants of the Chartist organization were ably assisting in the building up of the trades-unions; factory legislation, regulating the hours of employment and particularly child labor, was the first direct product of this agitation and growing consciousness. In Germany Ferdinand Lassalle was sounding the tocsin of proletarian action along class lines; and in France the activity of the workers' organizations, particularly in Paris, Lyons and other industrial centers, clearly betrayed an ever growing spirit of working-class solidarity.

This growing solidarity amongst the workers was stimulated and urged on to a more concrete manifestation, through the growing friendship and fraternal relations between the capitalists of various countries, an illustration of which was given at the second Universal Exhibition, held in London in 1862. This exhibition brought together a large number of business men and manufacturers from every nook and corner of the globe. And here, at receptions and banquets, the acquaintances were developed and the relations between the exploiters of the world solidified to such an extent that the exhibition became to be known amongst workingmen as the "International of the bourgeoisie." The supplement to this "International" was born, when on September 28th, 1864, workers' representatives from England, France, Germany, Poland and Italy gathered in St. Martin's Hall, London, and upon the proposal of the French delegate, M. Le Lubez, organized the proletarian expression of international solidarity under the name of the International Workingmen's Association—the first International.

Karl Marx actively participated in the preliminary work necessary for the calling of the conference. As the corresponding secretary for Germany, he was at the same time a member of the committee elected to draw up the constitution, programme or platform, etc., also to which the temporary management of the young organization's affairs was entrusted. Needless to say, the drafting of the association's declaration of principles and constitution was quite a delicate and complicated matter, and necessitated a thorough knowledge of working-class conditions in the different European countries. Furthermore, at that early state of capitalist development, relatively speaking of course, the programme of the International Workingmen's Association had to be formulated in such a manner as not to collide or be of hindrance to the different countries in their various stages of capitalist evolution. Under such manifold social and political conditions and at this particular period of capitalist development, the functions of the International could be at best only such of an advisory and educational capacity, and their effect in the main of a moral character. The International was to be a permanent or standing manifestation of the international solidarity of the proletariat, and its offices were to be employed to encourage, develop and cement these relations amongst the workers in the different countries wherever possible. Marx knew that only an internationally organized and class-conscious proletariat could hope to cope with and defeat the capitalist class and destroy the capitalist mode of production—an international institution; he also knew that organization and education of the workers would have to go hand in hand with the development of capitalism, if the workers were to achieve their end; he knew that no economic system ever disappeared or was relieved by another system until it had developed all faculties inherent in it; he, therefore, knew that tedious pioneer work would have to be done and that the social revolution was not to be accomplished via the route of conspiracy, spontaneous direct action of self-styled "minorities," assassination and bombastic phrase-mongery. Around what programmatic standard was the international proletariat to marshal its forces?

It was Marx who drafted both the constitution and the programme of the International Workingmen's Association, documents which were unanimously adopted by the organization. In the declaration of principles, better known as the "Inaugural Address," Marx outlined a plan of immediate action for the proletariat. This activity formed but "a part," to speak in the words of the "Address," "of the general struggle for emancipation of the toiling classes." The "Inaugural Address" was a child of the "Communist Manifesto." It also called attention to and emphasized the ever growing wealth in the hands of the possessing minority in society, and contrasts this with the ever increasing numbers in the propertyless working class and the increasing misery of this class, underscoring sharply the class antagonism between the exploiters and the exploited—an antagonism which is but the reflex of the economic divisions in capitalist society, divisions that are the original source of the social unrest. The "Inaugural Address" calls upon the workers to rise against misery and exploitation and advises them—fully appreciating the significance of the legal ten-hour day in England—to conduct this struggle via the road of independent political action and constructive, i. e., protective factory legislation; this activity was to be engaged in, however, always with the ultimate aim in view to conquer the political power for the proletariat in order to use the political machinery of the capitalist state to destroy forever all class rule. The document lays special weight upon the necessity of international working-class solidarity, a solidarity out of which an important duty arises, namely: to carefully control the foreign politics of the various capitalist governments, and to protest most emphatically and use all the might at the workers' command, should these politics pursue criminal aims, consciously exploit national prejudices and tend to squander the blood and possessions of the people in wars of conquest. When we read this passage in the light of the present war, then we can about perceive the significance of the warning: a warning which was, however, not heeded because the nationalism generated by the material conditions at the bottom of modern imperialism—understand full-fledged national capitalism—was able to even permeate the working-class movement, becoming for the time predominant in influence, even making international solidarity. ergo the class interests of the proletariat, subservient to its aim.

However, I am digressing from the subject proper. The principles and tactical suggestions just presented to you can be considered the basic aspirations and the ultimate and immediate aims of the first International at its inception. As the years of experience and constant struggle swept over this yet crude and immature class organization of the international proletariat, the clear-headed thinkers at its head were compelled to admit that the battle of the workers for emancipation was indeed an arduous struggle: a struggle which was inseparably interwoven with the development and perfection of the very system they, the proletarians, were destined to destroy. In the organization and growing class-consciousness of the proletariat is reflexed the organization and growing power of the capitalist system of production; the growth of one social layer compels the growth of the other, and just as intensive life foreshadows an early death, so does this social antithesis portend its culmination in the social revolution.

The process of economic evolution, with its accompanying class manifestations, is, however, as stated before, a tediously slow one. To the individual, conscious of his economic status and aware of the historic role the proletariat is to play in the future, social development seems stagnant and society intellectually corrupted or fossilized—dormant. To him the revolution is a mental reality, and could become a material one, if, yes, if the workers would only see the light and become class-conscious, i. e., would only become Socialists. The individual who reasons in this fashion, and who by the way is by no means a rarity in the movement of to-day, is everything but a Socialist in the Historical Materialistic, that is scientific conception of the term. He is a soaring idealist, who has lost the firm foundation of historical reality and material possibility from under his feet, and who is, consequently, utopistic in his deductions, actions and tactics. The first International, as is also the Socialist movement of to-day, was abundantly blessed with a large number of these undoubtedly sincere but intellectually ill-balanced comrades. Karl Marx and his followers, perceiving capitalist society through the spectacles of dialectical evolution and Historical Materialism, and seeing in all its manifestations but the logical sign of social development, were bound to collide with the gasconading idealist, who contemplated revolutionizing society via the road of back-room conspiracies and armed uprisings, especially at a time when sporadic prosperity had momentarily blinded the average wage slave to his actual conditions.

This struggle between Historical Materialism and utopian Idealism has been largely recorded by Socialist historians as a personal struggle between Marx and Bakunin for leadership in the International. Such writers are also everything else but Socialist historians, because if their conception were true, then the ghosts of Marx and Bakunin are at this advanced day still seeking to settle their personal quarrel in the Socialist and radical movement of every modern country on the face of the globe. The struggle between Historical Materialism, ergo scientific Socialism, and utopian Idealism—whether disguised as Opportunism, Impossibilism, Anarchist-Communism, etc., matters not— first took on shape and form in the first International and was led by Karl Marx and Michael Bakunin, respectively. It is not to be confused with the intellectual battle and polemics between scientific Socialism and the Utopianism of the French and English schools. As stated before, the intellectual struggle between these two conceptions is still going on in the movement, and will continue to go on until Historical Materialism or the Materialist Conception of History becomes the predominating conception in society—philosophically as well as socially: an intellectual revolution which we are rapidly approaching and which has its roots in the material conditions of capitalist production. The present world-war, I believe, has been a wonderful schoolmaster in this direction. Never were the interests, class aspirations and economic forces of the ruling classes and their pliable governments more openly exposed, and never have I read and perceived more articles and books, dealing with the economic and social aspects of the war, written and published by bourgeois members of society than since the outbreak of the war. Of course, in the Socialist movement the war has been also a great incentive to study and particularly to delve into the "mysteries" of the foundation of Scientific Socialism—the Materialist Conception of History.

To return to the subject. It cannot be denied, however, that the struggle between Historical Materialism and Utopian Idealism, as personified in Karl Marx and Michael Bakunin, tended gradually to disrupt the already loose form of the International's organization. This falling apart, however, carried within its womb the germs of consolidation and organization along national lines. And it is peculiar how the subsequent course of events furnished additional proof of the soundness of the Marxian method of historical analysis; for is it not indeed a striking coincidence only explainable with the aid of the Marxian key, when we perceive that in all countries with a prominent capitalist physiognomy, Marxism exercised full control in the organization, and in the Latin and chiefly agrarian countries Bakunism side by side with Marxism could be observed.

Then also capitalism was at this period commencing to carve out its national destiny in countries like Germany, France, Italy, the United States, etc., and in this process a series of so-called national problems was raised: problems, however, that had a disruptive influence and a disintegrating effect upon the International. In this connection I desire to cite the Franco-Prussian War which had resulted in the unification of the various German states and the organization of a powerful capitalist class in Germany. The reaction of the German conquests and annexation of Alsace-Lorraine, and the beastly crushing of the Paris Commune with the aid of Bismarck, had inflamed and aroused the national pride of the French people, and conjured the spectre of "revenge" upon the scene. England's undisturbed conquest of the world's markets, a conquest securely cemented by lucrative colonial possessions, had brought an era of prosperity to the British workers, of course relatively speaking; and the plan of the British imperialists to create a so-called world-empire, of course under the protectorate of Great Britain, a plan that was skilfully advocated by Lord Beaconsfield and that actually turned the heads of quite a few prominent men in the English labor movement, amongst them Joseph Cowen, who had been a strong supporter of the International, created such a spirit of jingoism in England and was productive of a national arrogance, which at this late day only finds its parallel in certain types of German workers.

These were the conditions and motives which prompted the Congress of the International at the Hague, in 1872, to transfer the seat of the organization's General Council to New York: a decision that in reality and practical effect actually implied the disbandment and the end of the International Workingmen's Association.

As a member of the General Council, Marx remained true to the International to the end. And to him the dissolution of this much-dreaded body implied only the reorganization of the proletarian forces on a larger and more class-conscious scale. The

"Inaugural Address" and "The Civil War in France" are two
historic publications and documents of the International Workingmen's Association of which he is the author, and which are
remarkable sign-posts of the proletariat's march to emancipation.
They are truly fitting supplements to the "Communist Manifesto." However, no one will ever know the volume of work performed by Marx as the so-called intellectual head of the International. Only a small portion of this activity is available in
documents. As a leader, educator and counsellor of leaders, he
performed invaluable services, not only while member of the
General Council, but up to his death. To one unfamiliar with the
conditions, the turbulent and primitive conditions that existed in
the early days of the modern labor movement, no adequate conception of the colossal magnitude of this task can present itself.
However, it is no exaggeration when I state, and my assertion is
based upon the reports of men who for years lived in intimate
association with Marx, that it was primarily this daily slew of
details, which steadily kept pouring in upon him from every nook
and corner of the globe and demanded his time and attention,
that prevented him from devoting his undivided energies to the
far more important scientific studies. Marx was a most conscientious student and advisor, and could devote days to research,
in order to furnish an authentic reply to an inquiry. Aside from
the historic causes cited above, here we have a tributary cause
responsible for Marx's retirement from leadership in the International—a retirement that fell together with the disintegration
of the organization. In just this energy-absorbing phase of
Marx's activity we can also locate the reason why on the day of
his death, March 14th, 1883, the second volume of "Capital" was
still uncompleted, and the material for the third volume had been
only collected and fragmentally suggested or roughly sketched in
his note book. However, to again quote Klara Zetkin: "The
principal work of Marx is comparable to a grand torso of antique
art, which even in its mutilated form speaks more impressively

and enchantingly to our soul than dozens of completed sculptures."

This presentation of the life and works of Marx would, however, be seriously defective, if no account of Marx's more intimate domestic life would be rendered, i. e., if that phase of life would be omitted which is really the basic element of all social activity—the every-day life. In order to do this intelligently, an understanding of the material conditions or social atmosphere in which he lived and of the characteristics of Marx and his inseparable companions is necessary.

Marx may truly and without indulging in platitudinous exaggerations be celebrated as an ideal type of revolutionist. He was, it is true, primarily a scientist; a scientist, however, who after having reached a definite deduction demanding a certain form of action did not shrink from the duty imposed upon him by scientific investigation and social circumstances, but cheerfully shouldered the task and unflinchingly labored to realize the demands of social evolution. Karl Marx was a true scientist, who did not consider himself a neutral and independent atom of the social organism—an atom that could function without affecting other atoms—but a scientist who through the result of his scientific findings felt himself morally compelled to participate in the reconstruction of society, who became a revolutionist, because he wanted to be and remain a true scientist. In Marx, therefore, the scientific world finds a man, who through his keen analysis and comprehension of social phenomena dedicated his faculties to the cause of the disinherited working-class; because, unlike so many of his contemporaries, he saw in that class the pioneer of all real progress, and also because to him the social interest was of far greater importance than his own material welfare. *He was a consistent revolutionist, because he sought to be and remain a consistent scientist.* Here we have a gratifying example where theory is supplemented by corresponding action: where a man's conduct squares with his principles. To Marx, scientific conviction and unhampered investigation were every-thing, and with sovereign scorn did he look down upon and treat that so numerous tribe of professorial scribes, who sell these in-dispensable prerequisites of liberty for the proverbial mess of pottage. And just because Marx was a searching scientist and his scientific findings made out of him a revolutionist, that is why he was ostracized by the class which to-day, by virtue of its eco-nomic power, is in control of the institutions of learning: that is why Marx was condemned to battle with the most dire poverty during the greatest part of his life.

To Marx, however, poverty was an incident of secondary importance and considered the legitimate product of a social manifestation of prime significance to him, and that was the movement—his ideal. Marx, like all great men of letters or geniuses, was a poor business man and an absolute failure as an administrator of the practical things in every-day life. To him life seemed to be a medium for the realization of certain aims and the promotion of the social welfare, and not an occasion for the talking of shop, the gratification of petty personal desires and the amassing of wealth, etc.

From the beginning of his exile in London and practically up to his death Marx and his family bore a burden of poverty far heavier and more unbearable than the one carried by the average proletarian family in those days. There were days in the Marx household when the stove was cold, the frost biting, the pantry empty and hunger upon the bill of fare; when the impatient land-lord stormed and threatened, and the children's starved faces and beseeching glances seemed to accusingly form themselves into a veritable indictment against their father. These ungrati-fying, yes, most miserable of miserable conditions pained Marx severely. Not because he feared or cared for material suffer-ings; no, Marx passed such vicissitudes of every-day life over with truly noble unconcern. What, however, affected and pained him so deeply was to see his wife, this faithful companion of his joyous boyhood days, and his beloved little ones suffer. Marx worshipped his wife and adored his children with a love and adoration that knew no bounds. And, therefore, when two of his daughters and his only son, his little Moosh, succumbed to this pitiful and devitalizing poverty, were, so to speak, sacrificed upon the altar of incorruptible and path-breaking science and to the cause of proletarian and social emancipation, his grief was uncontrollable and laid the foundation for his early and untimely death. From the death of his son, a child who bore the physical curse of poverty from the day of his birth until his death, he never recovered. In order that I may not awaken the feeling of doubt in my auditors or be charged with exaggeration, permit me herewith to quote a letter of Mrs. Marx to Mrs. Weydemeyer, the wife of an intimate friend of Marx residing in New York:

"My dear Mrs. Weydemeyer:

"In answer to your kind letter, which I received this morning, and in order to show you how delighted I was to receive it, I will write you a detailed letter at once, for now I see from your writing that you would like to hear from us, and that you have still preserved the same feelings of friendship as we have done.

"For how would it be possible for such old and tried comrades and friends, to whom Fate has given the same sufferings, the same pleasures, the same happy and sad days, ever to become strangers, though time and the ocean intervene? And so I extend my hand to you, as to a brave, true companion in adversity, a fellow struggler and sufferer. Yes, indeed, my dear Mrs. Weydemeyer, our hearts have often been filled with sorrow and gloom, and I can well imagine what you have had to contend with, again lately! I fully realize all you have to contend with, the cares and deprivations, for have I not often suffered the same! But suffering hardships and love gives strength.

"The first years of our life here were bitter ones, but I will not dwell on those sad memories to-day, on the losses we suffered, nor the dear, sweet departed children, whose pictures are engraved in our hearts with such deep sorrow.

"I will write of a newer period of our life rather, which, despite much sadness, has nevertheless, brought us many bright gleams of happiness.

"In 1856 I travelled to Trier with my three remaining daughters. My dear mother was overjoyed at our arrival, but, unfortunately, the joy was doomed to be of short duration. The most faithful, the best of mothers became ill and, after suffering for eleven days, closed her dear, tired eyes, her last glance resting fondly upon the children and me. Your dear husband, who knew what a loving mother she was, can best estimate my grief. We laid the dearly beloved body in its last resting place, and left Trier, after having settled the little legacy of my dear mother, dividing this equally between my brother Edgar and myself.

"Up to this time we had lived, in London, in two miserable rooms. We were now enabled, by means of the few hundred thalers my dear mother had left me, despite all the sacrifices she had made for us, to furnish a little house for ourselves, not far from the beautiful Hampstead Heath, and which we are still occupying. (As the translator of the "Woman in White," you will probably recall this name.)

"It is, truly, a princely dwelling, compared with our former narrow holes, and although the furnishing of the whole house cost us but forty pounds ('second-hand rubbish' playing the leading role) we felt quite 'high-toned,' possessing, as we did, a parlour. All the linen and other remnants of former greatness were now redeemed from the hands of the 'Uncle,' and it was a joy to me to be able to count my damask napkins of old Scotch origin once more. This grandeur, however, was of short duration, for soon afterward, one piece after the other had to wander back to the "Pop House" (as the children call the mysterious Three-Balls shop). Yet it gave us great pleasure to live once more in comparative comfort and ease.

"Then the first American crisis came and our income was cut in half. Our living expenses had to be screwed down once more, and we even had to incur debts. These had to be incurred in order to be able to continue the education of our girls further as begun.

"And now I come to the brightest part of our life, from which the only light and happiness was shed on our existence—our dear children. I feel certain that your husband, who was so fond of the girls when they were children, would be more heartily pleased with them now since they have grown into tall and blooming young women.

"Although I must fear that you will take me for a rather conceited and weak mother, I will give you a description of these dear praiseworthy girls. They are both exceptionally good-hearted, of generous dispositions, of truly amiable modesty and girlish purity. Jenny will be seventeen years of age on the first of May. She is a most charming girl, making quite a handsome appearance with her dark, shining, black hair and equally dark, shining soft eyes and her brunette, creole complexion with its acquired healthy English tints. The pleasant, good-natured expression of her round, childlike face makes one forget that she has a stub nose, which is perhaps not beautiful in itself, and it is a real pleasure when she speaks, to observe the friendly mouth with its fine teeth.

"Laura, who was fifteen years old last September, is perhaps prettier and of more regular features than her older sister, whose direct opposite she is. Although she is just as tall as Jenny, as slender and delicately formed, there is something lighter, brighter and more lucid about her. The upper part of her face may well be called beautiful with its waves of curly hair of chestnut brown, her sweet, dear eyes of changeable greenish lights that burn like triumphal fires, and her finely formed and noble forehead. The lower part of her face is less regular, being less developed. Both girls possess rosy, blooming complexions, and I often marvel at their lack of vanity, for I remember very well that the same could not have been said of their mother at a certain tender age!

"At school they have always carried off the first prizes. They are perfectly at home in English and are quite advanced in French. They are able to read Dante in Italian and also know a little Spanish; the German language seems to give them the greatest trouble; although I take every means in my power to prevail on them to take a German lesson now and then, my wishes do not always find obedience, so you see that respect for me and my authority are not very great. Jenny's special talent is for drawing, and the best ornaments in our home are her crayon drawings. Laura was so negligent about drawing that we had to deprive her of this instruction, as a punishment. She delights in practising on the piano, however, and sings charming English and German duets with her sister. Unfortunately, they commenced taking their musical instruction rather late, having begun only a year and a half ago. It had been impossible for us to raise the money for these expenses, for we had no piano. The one which we have now is only a hired one, and is old and dilapidated.

"The girls are a constant pleasure to us, owing to their affectionate and unselfish dispositions. Their little sister, however, is the idol of the whole house.

"This child was born at the time our poor, dear Edgar departed from life, and all our love for the little brother, all the tenderness for him, were now showered on the little sister, whom the older girls cherish with motherly solicitude. But you could scarcely find a lovelier child, so pretty, naive and full of droll humour is she. Her charming manner of speaking and relating stories is truly remarkable.' This she learned from the Grimm brothers, who are her companions by day and night. We all have read the fairy tales until we are almost blind, but woe to us if we were to forget one syllable of Rumpelstilzkin or Schneewittchen! By means of fairy stories, she has been able to learn the German language, which she speaks correctly besides the English language, which of course lies in the air. This little one is Karl's favourite pet, laughing and chatting away many of his troubles.

"I am happy in still having our dear, loyal, conscientious Lenchen to assist me in housekeeping; ask your dear husband about her, he will affirm what a treasure she is to us. For sixteen years she has faithfully stood by us through storm and adversity.

"Last year we had to suffer great annoyance from the infamous and vile attacks made by the whole German, American, etc., press. You have no idea how many sleepless nights and how much worry it all cost us. Our lawsuit against the *National-Zeitung* cost us a large sum of money, and when Karl had his book ready, he could find no publisher who would accept it. He finally had to have it published at his own expense (paying 25 pounds) and now after its appearance, the cowardly, corrupt press is trying to kill it by silence. I am delighted that you are pleased with the book. Your opinion is almost literally identical with that of all our other friends. Through the very intentional disregard of the book by the press, it could not reach the splendid sale which we had every right to expect.

"Meanwhile, the high approbation of all those of foremost intellectual standing must satisfy us. Our adversaries and enemies even have had to acknowledge its high value. Bucher described it as a compendium of the history of ages, and Lassalle writes that the enjoyment afforded him and his friends by this work of art was indescribable, and that their rejoicing and delight at so much wit was limitless. Engels considers this to be Karl's best book, as does 'Lupus.' Congratulations arrive from all sides, even our old enemy, Ruge, calls it a good farce. I am curious to see if America will observe the same silence. This would be actually revolting, after having given space to all those worthless lies and calumnies. Perhaps your dear husband could give some assistance in spreading its circulation.

"I had scarcely finished copying the manuscript, when I suddenly fell ill. A most terrible fever attacked me, and we had to send for a doctor. On the 20th of November he came, examined me carefully, and after keeping silent a long time broke out into the words: "My dear Mrs.

Marx, I am sorry to say you have got the smallpox—the children must leave the house immediately." You can imagine the distress and grief of the entire household at this verdict. What was to be done? The Liebknechts fearlessly offered to shelter the girls in their home, and by noon they had entered into exile, carrying their few belongings with them.

"I kept growing worse, hour after hour, the smallpox breaking out in the worst form. I suffered very, very much. Awful, burning pains in my face, complete sleepnessness, in deadly fear for Karl, who nursed me with the greatest tenderness, finally the loss of all senses save the inner sense of consciousness, which remained clear. I lay abed by the open window, so that the cold November air blew in upon me. At the same time there was a red hot fire in the stove; ice was placed upon my burning lips, and from time to time Bordeaux wine was infused in small quantities. I could hardly swallow, my hearing kept growing weaker, at last the eyes closed completely—who could tell if I should ever be able to see the light of day again?

"But my constitution was victorious, the tenderest, most faithful nursing assisted—and so I am sitting here again in complete health, but with disfigured face, marked by scars and a dark red coloring—quite *a la hauteur de la mode couleur de Magenta!* Christmas eve came and for the first time since my illness the poor children were allowed to return to their sadly missed home. This first meeting was indescribably pathetic. The girls were deeply affected and could hardly repress their tears when they saw me. But five weeks previous I had made quite an acceptable appearance beside my blooming daughters. Due to the surprising fact that I still had no gray hair and possessed good teeth and figure, I belonged to the class of well-preserved women—but now all this was gone! I felt as though I were a hippopotamus, belonging, rather to the Zoological Garden than to the Caucasian race. But do not let me frighten you too much. My appearance has improved quite a little, and the scars are beginning to heal.

"I had scarcely recovered sufficiently to be able to leave my bed, when my dearly beloved Karl took sick. Excessive fear, anxiety and vexations of every sort and description threw him upon his sick bed. For the first time, his chronic liver trouble had become acute. But thank heavens, he recovered after an illness of four weeks. In the meantime, the *Tribune* had placed us at half-pay again and, instead of getting some receipts from the book, we were obliged to meet a note. Added to this was the enormous expense of the most terrible of sicknesses. In short, you now have an idea how we fared last winter.

"As a result of all these affairs, Karl resolved to make a plundering expedition to Holland, the land of tobacco and cheese. He will endeavour to induce his uncle to help him out with money. So I am a grass widow at the present moment, and in high hope that the great Holland undertaking will be successful. Saturday of last week I received the first letter, which contained hopeful expressions and sixty gulden. Naturally, such a mission is not easily fulfilled; it takes time; one must be expedient, use diplomacy and be a good manager. I am in hopes, however, that Karl will drain Holland dry and leave the country poverty-stricken.

"As soon as he has attained success in Holland, he will undertake a secret trip to Berlin, in order to reconnoitre the conditions there with the possible plan of arranging for a weekly or monthly periodical. The latest experiences have convinced us only too well that no progress is possible without our own organ. If Karl's plan to create a new party paper succeeds, he will certainly write to your husband and call upon him for reports from America.

"Soon after Karl's departure, our faithful Lenchen took sick and to-day she is still abed, though on the road to recovery. For this reason I have my hands full of work, and have had to write this letter in the greatest of hurry. But I could not and would not remain silent any longer; it has been a great relief to me to unload my heart to my oldest, truest friends. I will not make any excuses to you for having written in detail of everything and everyone. My pen ran away with me, and I can only hope and wish that you may experience only a little of the pleasure I felt at reading your letter. I have already attended to the note and all is quite in order, just as though my lord and master were here.

"My girls send their heartiest greetings and kisses to your dear children—one Laura greets the other—and I kiss each one of them in spirit. To you, my dear friend, I send my warmest regards. May you remain brave and unshaken in these days of trial. The world belongs to the courageous. Continue to be the strong, faithful support of your dear husband and remain elastic in mind and body, the true 'unrespected' comrade of your dear children, and let me hear from you again at your first opportunity.   Yours in sincere friendship,

"Jenny Marx."

In the face of such cold, cruel and inhuman facts, in the presence of such unbearable misery, comment and critical appreciation become paralyzed: appalled by the shock inherent in this tragic revelation of a page in a man's life, who is to-day acclaimed and idolized as the formulator of a philosophical system for the proper conception of historical phenomena, and a pathfinder, if not the head, of modern Political Economy—who is considered the founder of a movement whose membership now runs into millions and which exercises a potential influence in every civilized country on the face of the globe! Any additional comment, in the face of such boundless and beautiful idealism and august devotion, seems sacrilegious and would only mar the profound impression created by this unpretentious narration of a phase in the life of this truly great and noble man. In conclusion I take the liberty to cite that well-known passage, a passage which is also quoted by Marx's daughter in closing her comment upon the turbulent life of her father:

> "the elements
> So mixed in him that Nature might stand up
> And say to all the world: 'This was a man'."

The next article in this series will be an essay on "An Outline for the Study of Marxism."

AN OUTLINE FOR THE STUDY
OF MARXISM

AN OUTLINE FOR THE STUDY OF MARXISM

A S a fitting supplement to the lectures published under this title in the first three numbers of this magazine, I will now endeavor to furnish the reader with a compilation of works which I deem absolutely essential for a serious and comprehensive study of Socialism. In the humble opinion of the writer, such a study must inevitably lead to a scientific understanding of Marxism—an understanding quite imperative to an intelligent and sound appreciation of Capitalism.

There is probably no social theory outside of the various religious conceptions, and no book except the Bible that can boast of more adherents and advocates the world over than Socialism and "Capital." Socialism is to-day a factor in the social and political life of every nation, and the theoretical propositions and basic principles of Marxism are at this turbulent period the revolutionary force and intellectual standard around which the workers and all truly disinterested students of Sociology and Political Economy rally in their struggle against the debasing influences of the mercenary Social Sciences. Marxism can, therefore, and without indulging in exaggeration, lay claim to the legacy of Classical Political Economy, and consider itself the *only* legitimate heir to the scientific values of this science. And acting in accord with this dictate of social development, Marx has raised upon the solid foundation laid by a Petty, Smith, Ricardo and Mills a structure truly massive, colossal and inspiring in its mighty grandeur, and overpoweringly convincing, yes unassailable and irrefutable in the scientific profundity of its construction.

As has been amply elucidated and sufficiently explained, the two propositions upon which the theoretical system of Marx rests and whose proper appreciation is absolutely necessary for a thorough and rational understanding of Marxism are the Materialist Conception of History and the Socialist critique and analysis of capitalist production, or Capitalism. I have dwelt at length upon these two fundamental phases of Socialist letters in my lectures, and, therefore, do not consider it essential to enter upon a discussion of them here, or to even emphasize the importance of their proper study and assimilation.

Every scientist will concede that the basis for a competent understanding of or mastery over any branch of learning rests solely in systematic study and the well organized classification and application of the knowledge or subject matter absorbed. Socialism is no exception to the rule. For a thorough knowledge of the elements of Socialist Philosophy and Economics a well planned and systematically executed course of critical reading and diligent study is absolutely essential. Such a course of reading and study is, however, taking the present conditions in the field of Socialist literature as a criterion, not so easily compiled; especially, if the prospective student attempts to perform this task himself, i. e., without procuring the advice or counsel of a competent authority. In no field of intellectual endeavor or pursuit, in no science are there more snares, snags and traps awaiting the unwary and trusting student than in the field of theoretical Socialism. And when we view the innumerable collections of irresponsible, defective, yes in many cases fundamentally erroneous works which are daily offered to the public as "recognized textbooks" on Socialism, then we can easily account for this ungratifying situation and also readily explain the Babylonian confusion and criminal inconsistency at times rampant in the Socialist movement. Furthermore, when perceiving that such "textbooks," which in the most cases are at best only unquestionable testimonials of their author's ignorance of Socialism, are circulated by responsible agencies in the Socialist Party, then the unbiased Socialist, to whom clarity in Socialist letters is more than a cherished aspiration, must confess that it certainly is not such a simple task after all for the un-initiated seeker to arrive at a clear and scientific conception of Marxism.

I believe I am not exaggerating when I state that no movement has placed its founder upon a higher pedestal, or paid a greater tribute to its master than the Socialist movement. If anyone desires to view an example of deep gratitude and noble affection let him study the whole-hearted idolization of Karl Marx indulged in by the proletariat the world over. There is no civilized country upon the globe in which there are not hundreds of thousands of workingmen who proclaim themselves adherents to Marx's teachings. The picture of this great thinker adorns the parlor of every Socialist home, and can be found in every Socialist or trades-union hall. His masterpiece and textbook of scientific Socialism, "Capital," enjoys the undivided admiration of *all* Socialists. Be they orthodox revolutionists or plastic opportunists matters not, in the laudation of Marx and his works they are one and claim to be—Marxists. Another peculiarity, which has its origin in the object to exploit the international reputation of Marx for political purposes, is the persistency of Socialist organizations or factions with the most conflicting principles to proclaim their position to be in conformity with Marxian precepts, or to be the only "true" Marxian position. Consequently, since the death of Marx, the most farcical and disgusting political campaigns and pillaging expeditions have been labelled or masqueraded in the guise of Marxism, and are even at this late day usurping the name of the great master for the purpose of political capital. These unsavory tactics and ungratifying conditions are made possible and tolerated in the Socialist movement, because the reverence entertained for and unbounded confidence placed in Marx are not predicated upon a sound knowledge of or an even superficial familiarity with the actual works of this celebrated economist. There is probably no book in the scientific literature of the world that enjoys greater popularity, is more appealed to, oftener recommended and less read than "Capital." In consequence, it will be difficult to find another science, enjoying the same popularity as Marxism, in whose name are propagated so many conflicting and erroneous views. As already insinuated, the cause for these ungratifying conditions can be traced to the colossal ignorance prevalent amongst so-called "Marxian" Socialists on matters Marxian. Therefore, the only force able to curb and eventually obliterate "these evil powers of darkness" is familiarity with the works of their idol, and an acquaintance with the lucid teachings of their much heralded leader, through a systematic study of Socialist classics. The organization of classes or circles for the study of Socialist classics should, consequently, be seriously taken in hand by all Socialists who have the healthy development of Marxism at heart. A vigorous, revolutionary political and industrial movement of Socialism can only flow from a sound theoretical conception of Marxism; no conscious, effective and revolutionary policy can be expected from the vast majority of the political and economic forces now operating under the banner of Socialism.

*   *   *

When a student enters upon the study of Socialism, the first truism he should remember is that Socialism as a science does not occupy itself nearly so extensively with the contemplation and elucidation of future society, as with the examination and economic analysis of the present one. Scientific Socialism is, therefore, not as it is generally and mistakenly assumed, a theoretical system dealing *solely* with the multifarious phases of the Cooperative Commonwealth, but one which constitutes *primarily* an inquiry into the origin, foundation, laws and tendencies noticeable in the development of capitalist production. In consequence, a knowledge of Socialism does not consist of an individual's competence to memorize a definition formulating the economic and social basis of Socialist production, i. e., setting forth the economic groundwork of the Industrial Republic and the social consequences resulting therefrom, but rather of his ability to file a brief for Socialism, by convincingly pointing out the necessity for and inevitability of the Cooperative Commonwealth germinating in the womb of capitalist society. A knowledge of Socialism demands, therefore, in the first place not so much a study of future society as it does a thorough investigation of present social and economic life. In consequence, Socialism represents more an investigation of capitalist production and an exposition of the social and economic laws underlying the same than an abstract theory or speculation of Industrial Democracy. However, it must be also emphasized that in order to have a normal, that is scientifically sound conception of future society, and an understanding of the forces and social elements making for it, a deep and scientific appreciation of Capitalism is absolutely indispensable.

As an excellent introduction into the so-called mysteries of Economics and the peculiarities of the Socialist nomenclature, also as a textbook of Socialism unparalleled for lucidness, pithiness and accuracy I recommend a close study of "Das Erfurter Programm," by Karl Kautsky, published in English complete under the name of "The Class Struggle" and translated by Wm. E. Bohn, or chapters of which are issued in pamphlet form under the titles of "The Working Class," "The Capitalist Class," "The Class Struggle" and "The Socialist Republic," translated and adapted to American conditions by Daniel De Leon. There is probably no book in the by no means limited assortment of Socialist literature that equals this work in its scrupulous accuracy of exposition; an accuracy made doubly effective because it is coupled with a remarkable and rare simplicity in the presentation of Marxian fundamentals. Here we have a compendium of Socialism, written by a Marxian scholar of international repute, classical in its treatment of the subject matter, and truly deserving the widest possible circulation in the Socialist and labor movement. "Das Erfurter Programm," as the German title of "The Class Struggle" suggests, was originally written to furnish a theoretical explanation and scientific elucidation of the programme of the German Social Democracy, adopted at Erfurt, 1891, to the workers. The very purpose and nature of such a work makes out of it a rich source of information for particularly the serious student; because here the penetrating rays of Marxism are thrown upon the programmatic demands and principles of a political party of Socialism, and employed or utilized to verify the same before the bar of science. "Das Erfurter Programm" ("The Class Struggle") succeeds admirably in presenting and explaining Socialist fundamentals to the novice or uninitiated. However, in doing this, it claims to be, as already stated, substantiating the demands and theoretical propositions laid down in the Erfurt programme of the Social Democratic Party. In the opinion of the writer, the object of this splendid work has been only partially fulfilled, at least the object of its publishers, because as an advocate of sound, scientific fundamentals it has no rival in Socialist literature, in consequence, neither can it find its equal as a repudiator of palliatives and so-called immediate demands, so popular in the German Social Democracy and with which the Erfurt programme is overloaded.

Possessing a working knowledge of the genesis and character of capitalist production, also of the economic and social status of the various classes in present society, the student should now seek to familiarize himself more thoroughly with the Socialist conception of social evolution, i. e., with the philosophical foundation of scientific Socialism. Familiarity with the elements and propositions of Historical Materialism will also lead to a better understanding and more competent appreciation of social phenomena, and simultaneously equips the reader with the knowledge that will henceforth enable him to differentiate intelligently between Utopian and Scientific Socialism. An intensive study of Frederick Engels' masterpiece "Development of Socialism from Utopia to a Science" is now recommended. In conjunction with these philosophical studies, the student ought to read the "Preliminary Remarks" to "Principles of Political Economy," by John Stuart Mills. In this introduction the great English Economist gives in a lucid and brilliant form a short resumé of the principal stages in the evolution of the human race. If this work is not procurable, then the student can commence immediately with the "Evolution of Property," by Paul Lafargue. However, a diligent perusal of Mills' "Preliminary Remarks" can not be too strongly recommended.

In order to develop and broaden the student's knowledge of Political Economy, the study of the following works is now opportune and must be carried out in the order they are listed: "Wage, Labor and Capital," by Karl Marx; "High Cost of Living," by Arnold Petersen; "Value, Price and Profit," by Karl Marx.

Knowing the economic and social forces underlying social development, also possessing a scientific conception of social phenomena and historical manifestations; furthermore, being somewhat familiar with the general phases of social evolution, it is now desirable and quite essential that the student begin a somewhat systematic study in Ethnology, Sociology and History. As an introduction to this interesting course of reading, the student should slowly and patiently explore that treasure island of facts, that monumental work in Ethnology, "Ancient Society," by Lewis H. Morgan. A thorough and diligent study of this classic is absolutely imperative and will greatly assist in the proper understanding of the subsequent periods in historical development. A study of the following works is now recommended: "The Ancient Lowly," by C. Osborne Ward; "Two Pages from Roman History," by Daniel De Leon; "Crises in European History," by Gustav Bang; "An Introduction to the Study of the Middle Ages" and "Medieval Europe," by Ephraim Emerton; "The Middle Ages," by Henry Hallam; "History of European Morals," by William Edward Hartpole Lecky; "General History of Civilization in Europe," by Francois Pierre Guillaume Guizot; "History of Civilization in England," by Henry Thomas Buckle; and as supplementary reading "The Mysteries of the People, or History of a Proletarian Family Across the Ages," by Eugene Sue, translated from the original French by Daniel De Leon. The last work by Sue in this series consists of 21 volumes, and is really a universal history in itself, depicting the class struggle as it has raged through the ages and under the different social systems. For a study of social development in America the works listed below will be found suitable; these works are written by scholars well ground in the theories of Historical Materialism, and, consequently lay bare the actual driving forces responsible for and behind social change in this country: "American Industrial Evolution from Frontier to Factory," by Justus Ebert; "Social Forces in American History," by A. M. Simons; and "The Workers in American History," by James Oneal.

It is now also necessary that the student acquaint himself with the inception and growth of the Socialist movement, a growth, however, that has not always kept abreast with the development of theoretical Socialism. The following classics of Socialist literature and historic documents should now be critically read: "The Communist Manifesto," by Karl Marx and Frederick Engels; "Revolution and Counter-Revolution, or Germany in 1848," erroneously credited to and published under the name of Karl Marx, but actually written by Frederick Engels; "The Class Struggle in France 1848-1850," by Karl Marx; "The Eighteenth Brumaire of Louis Napoleon," by Karl Marx; and "The Civil War in France" ("The Paris Commune"), by Karl Marx. In conjunction with the foregoing the following works, dealing in the main with American conditions and problems, may be profitably read: "History of Socialism in the United States," by Morris Hillquit; "Proceedings of the Ninth Convention of the S. L. P."; "Proceedings of the Tenth National Convention of the S. L. P., 1900"; "New Jersey Socialist Unity Conference";

"Flashlights of the Amsterdam Congress," by Daniel De Leon; "Launching of the I. W. W.," by Paul F. Brissenden; and "Proceedings of the First Convention of the Industrial Workers of the World, Chicago, 1905."

Fully equipped with the various subjects and phases constituting the theoretical system of Marxism, and being also somewhat familiar with the various stages and periods of social development, the student is now amply prepared to take up the study of works usually considered too ponderous or "academic" for the unprepared worker. These works form the basis of the theoretical structure of Marxism, and their study is, therefore, synonymous with imbibing the Socialist philosophy at its "original sources." The first of this class of works to be assiduously studied is Frederick Engels' "Landmarks of Scientific Socialism" (Anti-Duehring). In conjunction with this invaluable gem of Socialist literature "Feuerbach, Roots of Socialist Philosophy," by the same author; and "A Critique to Political Economy" and "Poverty of Philosophy," by Karl Marx should be read; special attention being given to the Preface of the "Critique." In this connection "The Theoretical System of Karl Marx," by Louis B. Boudin, will also serve as very effective and profitable supplementary reading.

The next and final work to be taken up in this course of reading will be the study of "Capital," the so-called foundation or basic work of Socialist Political Economy. Before, however, commencing this important and tedious task, the student should do some additional preliminary reading and rehearse his studies in Economics. He should, for example, reread "Wage, Labor and Capital," "Value, Price and Profit," etc., and particularly seek to master the contents of Marx's "A Critique to Political Economy," already referred to above. Furthermore, a perusal of works of a critical and more or less controversial nature, occupying themselves with the various phases of Marxism as formulated and substantiated in "Capital," will be of great assistance to a proper understanding of this masterpiece. For this purpose, the following brochures are recommended as collateral reading: "Vulgar Economy," by Daniel De Leon; "Marx on Mallock, or Facts versus Fiction," by the same author; "Was Marx Wrong?", by I. M. Rubinow; and "Karl Marx and Boehm-Bawerk, Vulgar Economy Illustrated," by W. H. Emmett.

The study of "Capital" can now be taken up, and in this connection the following suggestions should be observed. The social and historical significance of this work has been, I believe, sufficiently emphasized and dealt with in the lectures proper and, therefore, requires no further elucidation. What is now of prime importance to the prospective reader or student of "Capital" is a plan or course of procedure netting the best possible results with the smallest expenditure of energies. It can not be denied, all popular assertions notwithstanding, that "Capital" is to the average workingman, unaccustomed to scientific works, quite a tedious and ponderous volume; furthermore, that an indiscriminate and unsystematic reading of this book is not very conducive to either the spirit and future efforts of the reader, or to an intelligent appreciation of the work itself. As underscored in this article before, in the humble opinion of the writer, an EXHAUSTIVE course of preliminary reading and study is absolutely essential, yes, a prerequisite, for a proper understanding of "Capital." Hence if classes or individuals, not equipped with the aforementioned knowledge so necessary for a proper perception or understanding, i. e., unprepared and untrained to assimilate or digest the intellectual food offered in this monumental work, give up their studies in despair, then the reason should not be ascribed to the "ponderous form of presentation in 'Capital'," but to the insufficient preparation and inability of these students to understand the nature and mode of Marx's investigations and deductions. However, those who have diligently followed the lecturer through his discourses and studied the books recommended in this Outline need have no fears on this score, and will experience no difficulties in understanding "Capital."

To the student desirous of conserving energy, also to the teachers of "Capital" I would suggest and warmly recommend that they begin the study of the book not in the customary way, but commence with Part VIII, The So-Called Primitive Accumulation. This section deals with and graphically depicts the social and economic origin of capital and capitalist production, and shatters once and for all time that well-known myth of capital being the result or fruit of abstinence. In a powerful and highly fascinating style, Marx unrolls before the eyes of the reader a picture vividly showing the birth, development and culmination of Capitalism. Here we have a history of the capitalistic stage in the endless chain of social development, a history written by the formulator of Historical Materialism, and it is truly a presentation throbbing with the creative vitality only inherent in convincing and irrefutable arguments: arguments taken from and corresponding with the indisputable facts of historic data and events. In this section of the book the secret of primitive accumulation, the expropriation of the peasants and their dispossession from the soil, the bloody and barbarous legislation against the expropriated in the 15th, 16th and 17th Centuries, the genesis of agrarian and industrial capital, and the historical tendencies of capitalist accumulation are exposed and dispassionately analyzed; including a scientific dissection of our modern theory of colonization—an examination that will prove to be particularly interesting when read in the light of the present war.

From this part of the book turn to Part III, Chapter X, on The Working Day, and read Section 1, The Limits of the Working Day, Section 2, The Greed for Surplus Labor.—Manufacturer and Boyard, Section 3, Branches of English Industries without Legal Limits to Exploitation, Section 4, Day and Night Work.— The Relay System, Section 5, The Struggle for a Normal Working Day.—Compulsory Laws for the Extension of the Working

Day from the Middle of the 14th to the End of the 17th Century, Section 6, The Struggle for the Normal Working Day.—Compulsory Limitation by Law of the Working Time.—The English Factory Acts, 1833 to 1864, Section 7, The Struggle for a Normal Working Day.—Reaction of the English Factory Acts on Other Countries. As the sub-headings sufficiently indicate, this chapter deals solely with the historical growth of and tendencies developed by capitalist exploitation, and thus furnishes an indictment of fact fearlessly laying bare the revolting, barbarous and anti-social character of the capitalist system of production.

In order to refresh the student's memory along the lines of the Materialist Conception of History, and for the purpose of familiarizing him with a brilliant piece of applied Historical Materialism, he should turn to Part IV, and assiduously peruse Chapter XV, dealing with Machinery and Modern Industry. In this chapter the following interesting problems are taken up: The Development of Machinery, The Value transferred by Machinery to the Product, The Proximate Effects of Machinery on the Workman (Appropriation of Supplementary Labor-Power by Capital, The Employment of Women and Children, Prolongation of the Working Day, Intensification of Labor), The Factory, The Strife between Workman and Machinery, The Theory of Compensation as regards Workpeople displaced by Machinery, Repulsion and Attraction of Workpeople by the Factory System, Revolution effected in Manufacture, Handicrafts, and Domestic Industry by Modern Industry, The Factory Acts, etc., and Modern Industry and Agriculture.

Being fully acquainted with the origin, development and tendencies of Capitalism, also quite familiar with the historical role assumed by it in the process of social evolution, the student is now sufficiently equipped to study the economic structure and laws of the capitalist system of production. And to this phase of investigation the remaining and largest part of "Capital" is devoted. Having digested such works as "Value, Price and

Profit," "The Class Struggle," "A Critique to Political Economy," etc., the student is well ground and at home in the Socialist and scientific terminology, also in the elements of Marxian Economics, and should, therefore, experience no difficulties in the study of such portions of the work dealing primarily with the investigation and analysis of capitalist production in its pure economic form. The first Chapter of Part I can be defined as the bedrock of Socialist Economics. In the four sections composing this masterly treatise on Commodities, the basic principles and substance of Marxian Economics are laid down. In this chapter such highly important subjects as The two Factors of a Commodity, Use Value and Value (the Substance of Value and the Magnitude of Value), The Twofold Character of the Labor embodied in Commodities, The Form of Value or Exchange Value and The Fetishism of Commodities are subjected to an examination, the findings resulting therefrom elucidated and formulated in concise statements and accurate deductions. A mastery of the first ninety-six pages of "Capital" is, consequently, essential for an intelligent understanding of the remaining chapters in the book; because such a mastery equips the student with a faculty of scientific conception and differentiation quite conducive and necessary to further progress; again, the fact of being at home in the labyrinth of theoretical definitions and economic complexities constituting the groundwork of Marxian Economics is in itself an invaluable asset to the future intellectual labors of the student, and implies, without exaggeration, a knowledge of the quintessential principles of Marxism. Once the student has a correct conception of such familiar terms as Wealth, Value, Use Value, Exchange Value, Commodity, Labor Power, Surplus Value, Capital, etc., the hardest or most irksome part of the task can be considered accomplished. The remaining chapters in the work can now be taken up and studied in their regular order, including a re-reading of those previously studied, and the student should, relatively considered, experience no exceptional difficulties in his work.

To not a few readers this course of study will no doubt seem ponderous and unnecessarily voluminous. It will probably strike many as being too "academic," "theoretical" and "impractical." The absence of the current and popular works and tracts on Socialism may also seem inexplicable to some and earn for this course the reputation of being too "scientific" or "orthodox." To all these antiquated and well known but superficial criticisms and stereotype platitudes the author has only one reply to make, namely: that the above is to be a course in Marxian Socialism, aiming solely to equip the students with a working knowledge of the fundamentals and basic elements of the Socialist philosophy. It is not to be a course in the various "adaptations" and "practical" revisions or abortions of Marxism, popularly taught to a naive and guileless public as "scientific" Socialism by a set of unscrupulous political fakirs. All the works listed and recommended in this course are recognized classics of Socialism, and can be considered as standing proof for the absolute superfluousness of the countless collection of books and pamphlets published on this subject, all claiming to be "popular expositions" of Socialism and "filling a long felt want." Most of these works contain as a rule nothing else but the intellectual drivel of a coterie of, in many cases, well meaning but ignorant pseudo intellectuals, and in other instances may be classified as the output of a set of unprincipled mercenaries, who see in the labor and Socialist movement a lucrative field for the realization of their personal ambitions. Therefore, the author sincerely trusts that the perusal and diligent study of the works listed in this course will assist to create a sound conception of Marxism and a demand for scientific SOCIALIST literature in the Socialist movement.

*   *   *

In the essay entitled "The Constructive Elements of Socialism," the author has attempted to combine Marxism proper with the tactical and constructive phases of Socialism as they exist in the modern labor movement and are necessitated or produced by the social forces inherent in modern and full-fledged Capitalism. This essay also concludes this series, and can be considered the practical application of revolutionary Marxism to oligarchic, imperialistic Capitalism.

THE CONSTRUCTIVE ELEMENTS
OF SOCIALISM

I.

IT is a recognized and accepted proposition amongst Socialists that Socialism derives its claim to a science from two branches of scientific investigation: The first, Marxian Economics, is a thorough dissection and profound critique of capitalist production; and the second, the Materialist Conception of History, provides the student with a theory for the understanding and appreciation of historical phenomena or social development.

Through the application of the Socialist method of historic investigation to social evolution, the various and ever changing stages in the complex development of mankind assume a more distinct form, and the driving forces and causes underlying this endless chain of struggles, transformations and revolutions are laid bare and exposed to the investigator. Through the proper utilization of the Materialist Conception of History in studying the past and present of human progress, history, with its many almost impenetrable mysteries and strange labyrinths, ceases to be a closed book to the student, and becomes a vital, interesting narrative, depicting the unceasing struggles of the classes through the ages: a struggle that finds its culmination in the furious class war raging between Capital and Labor to-day, and that will be definitely concluded with the abolition of class prerogatives in property and the establishment of the Industrial Republic. As stated before, to shed light on the multifarious phases of historical development, and to thus enable the investigator to intelligently appreciate and appraise existing conditions by a sound knowledge of the past, also to enable him to vision and penetrate into the future with the aid of scientific spectacles, that is the domain of Historical Materialism, the groundwork of the Socialist philosophy.

Upon this massive and imposing foundation the system of Socialist, or, to be more exact, Marxian Economics is erected. The Economics of Marx are nothing else but a key for the proper understanding of the origin, nature and culmination of the capitalist system of production. Marxian Economics furnish to the student a complete analysis of the laws underlying present-day production; they point out the causes of the various industrial manifestations and also expose and formulate the tendencies inherent in these economic potentialities. Thus the genesis of profit, interest, rent, unemployment, panics, competition and wars is easily ascertained with the aid of the Marxian system of economic research. For a scientific conception of Capitalism, therefore, the study of Socialist Economics is indispensable. *And without a sound knowledge of capitalist production, no effective* Socialist activity, economic or political, is possible.

The Materialist Conception of History and Marxian Economics, i. e., the Socialist conception of historic development plus the Socialist analysis of capitalist production, these two theoretical systems are the intellectual pillars upon which the Socialist movement rests—they symbolize the bedrock of Socialist science. In proportion as the Socialist movement organizes and develops in accord with the dictates flowing from a proper assimilation of these principles, in that proportion will it become a *Socialist* movement and possess the revolutionary and constructive vitalities so peculiar to a class-conscious movement, and vice versa. Therefore the strength of the Socialist movement is necessarily to be found in a sound and comprehensive understanding of its principles and aims by the rank and file. Without this understanding no intelligent action is possible, and no responsible opinion can be rendered or decision arrived at. Consequently, familiarity with the fundamentals of the Socialist philosophy is an imperative prerequisite for a competent conception of party problems, and also for the proper understanding of Socialist tactics.

The question of Socialist tactics belongs to the Constructive Department of Socialism. It is a question which is generally raised unwillingly, and mostly considered not worthy of serious discussion. To many Socialists, and they are generally of the calibre who have not mastered the fundamental prerequisites underscored above, the tactics of the Socialist movement are not determined by the conscious efforts of the Socialists, but are more or less the products of chance. And when we study the tactics employed by the different state and local organizations of the Socialist Party in this country, and notice the different conceptions responsible for the same—conceptions that, in many cases, go as far apart as day and night—then we must conclude: that this melting pot of tactics, this tactical hash, is only conceivable and possible in an organization whose members have as yet developed *no unity of opinion as to the aim and historic mission of Socialism.* A proper conception of the social significance of Capitalism, coupled with a knowledge of the economic structure or capitalist production, is bound to equip every worker with a proper understanding of the role played, or to be played by the Socialist movement in present society. Such an understanding will necessarily and instinctively stimulate the imagination, and create a vision of the goal of the Socialist movement in the mind of every proletarian. The historic role and status, and the goal of the Socialist movement being given, the determination of the proper tactics and methods to be employed in the struggle for industrial liberty now becomes imperative and a burning question.

*   *   *

The Constructive Department of Socialism is that branch of Socialist philosophy which occupies itself with the methods and forms of organization to be employed by the workers in their struggle against the exploiters for the Industrial Republic. It is the logical supplement to the two theoretical systems touched upon above; Marxian Economics and Historical Materialism emphasizing the necessity for and historic basis of Socialism, and Constructive Socialism pointing out the method for its realization. This constructive phase of Socialism is in reality the most important element in the Socialist philosophy, because the development and success of the class-conscious proletariat actually depend upon its proper organization and the correct tactical interpretation and application of Socialist principles. Without the proper appreciation of the Socialist goal and adoption of the tactics resulting therefrom, no decisive victory for the working class is possible—no victory for Socialism can be obtained. The tactics, nature and form of organization of the Socialist movement may, therefore, be defined as the tools of the working class absolutely essential to the erection of the Industrial Republic. To determine and define these methods and forms of proletarian organization is, consequently, synonymous with laying the theoretical foundation of the Socialist Commonwealth.

Marxian Economics clearly emphasize that the capitalist system will only disappear with the abolition of private ownership in the means of production. This proclaims the necessity for industrial revolution. The basis of Capitalism is private ownership, consequently, the basis of Socialism, its antithesis, can only be social ownership; as can readily be seen—one excludes the other, and the domination of one implies the subjugation of the other. Industrial revolution or the movement for industrial revolution, can, therefore, project only one demand and that is the socialization of industry and all agencies of production. Such a demand, however, is not only in accord with the tendencies and dictates of social evolution, but also voices at the same time the specific class interests of the proletariat, and can, therefore, only emanate from that social layer. The demand of social evolution, whose obedient servant the working class is, is a demand at war with the basic interests of the capitalist class. The working class, as an agent of social evolution, and the capitalist class, as an obstacle in the path of economic progress, have, therefore, *nothing in common.* This fundamental difference of interests, functions and historic destinies breeds the class antagonism and the struggle for power.

To-day Capitalism is strongly fortified behind economic and political bulwarks. By virtue of its industrial powers, it has humanity the world over at the throat. To dislodge Capitalism from this powerful position, and to thus lay the cornerstone of the Socialist Commonwealth is the august mission of Constructive Socialism.

In this struggle between the capitalist class and the proletariat, the latter, being in the position of aggressor, is naturally at a disadvantage. It is a disadvantage, however, that compels a survey of the battlefield by the workers, the results of which contain the solution to the problem of how to overcome and eliminate this obstacle. This survey of the economic, political and social position of the capitalist class reveals, that the basic power or influence of this class resides not, as is so often erroneously assumed, in its political domination or control of government, but *in its economic rule over society.* History teaches and profusely illustrates: that the class in control of the economic resources of society in a given period has also been the class to exercise practical control over political society, i. e.—over society itself. History vindicates the contention that the economic life of society, the form of ownership and methods of production and exchange existing at a certain stage of social development, is the compelling factor, the preponderant form, which determines, influences and shapes all other ethical, moral, intellectual and political, in short—cultural phases of life.

A casual study of the periods of Antique Slavery, Feudalism and Capitalism will serve to convincingly illustrate this contention. Such a study will reveal that the roots of Slavery rested in the absolute domination of a people by another; that the enslavement and exploitation of a people by Rome was made possible only by the superior and well organized economic resources and

the disciplined armies of the conquerors. The economic foundation
of Rome was predicated on organized slavery; and even the
classic period of Letters and Art in Greece and Rome, that as
yet uneclipsed period of splendour, was reared upon the backs of
slaves. With the decay and fall of Slavery, the marvellous splendour, and the political and military power of Rome also collapsed.
The same tendencies are also detectable when examining Feudalism. Here we note the unlimited power of social control vested
in the same feudality, which through its ownership or tenure of
the land—the then main agent of production—exerted practically
an undivided influence over every detail in the life of its subjects.
By virtue of this economic control—land ownership—the feudal
lord was actually elevated to the position of arbitrator over the
life, happiness and prosperity of his serfs: He held their destinies
in the hollow of his hand, because he monopolized the wherewith
of life—the land. And when we make an investigation of Capitalism, the by far preponderant role played by the economic
element of the capitalists' power in present society is easily dis-
cernible. Here we are compelled to admit that the class divisions
of to-day, similar to the ones of yore, are fundamentally economic
or property divisions. Furthermore, that the influence of a class
is not measured by the degree of its productivity, or the proportion of its work for the social welfare, etc., but mainly by the
economic power in its control. To illustrate, in society to-day the
nigh illimitable and colossal dimensions of the workers' productive faculties are easily recognized and acknowledged by everyone.
At the same time the relatively insignificant and minor role played
by the capitalists in this industrial process is well known. If
social and political influence were apportioned in ratio to the
economic use-value of a class, then the proletariat would certainly
be the dominant class in society and the capitalists occupy a most
insignificant position. The opposite being the case, proves con-
clusively that political and social influence is not the fruit of social
service, but the product, as was the case in previous centuries, of
economic power in some shape or form. The economic power of

the capitalist class, a power to which the vast majority of the population is compelled to pay homage, is not only lodged in the private ownership of land, as in the case of Feudalism, but in the private ownership of *all* instruments and agencies of wealth production. The title of private ownership to the means necessary to the life and prosperity of a nation, vested in a numerically insignificant minority, gives this minority an unlimited control over the welfare and happiness of a people. Here we have the source of capitalist power—the genesis of the social and political significance of the capitalist class. The title of private ownership in the means of production is the cornerstone of the capitalists' social influence—*the generator of every form of capitalist power*.

To shatter this foundation of capitalist class might, to capture this stronghold of industrial despotism in the interest of the workers, must, therefore, be the one great object of Constructive Socialism. The destruction of the economic power of the capitalist class, of course, also spells the collapse of its political rule, together with the social position occupied by this class, and announces the inception of the social revolution and the elevation of all the producers in society to the rulership of society. The question how to organize the proletarian forces for this momentous and gigantic object; how to create the so essential power in the working class; this question is now in order, and its proper solution forms the quintessence of Constructive Socialism—the basis for scientific Socialist tactics and effective action.

* * *

It is a recognized truism that pressure begets pressure and that might breeds might. Furthermore, must the inexorable fact be recognized that the means and tactics of warfare of the aggressor, in this case the proletariat, are largely dependent on and determined by the strategical position and general methods employed by the enemy, the capitalist class. A study of the social position of the capitalist class has already revealed to us that the roots of the exploiters' power in society are to be found in their economic control of the socially necessary means of production. The holding of this economic citadel imparts a strength or power to the capitalist class phenomenal in scope and only explainable by the absolute indispensability of these economic resources to society. To capture this position from the capitalist class; *to meet the economic power of the plutocrats with a superior economic power of the workers,* that is the next logical step in this gigantic struggle.

Economic power, as has been sufficiently illustrated in the foregoing pages, is the source of all other forms of social influence; therefore, economic power can be correctly defined *as the basic element of social might.* Consequently, if a class seeks to rise to political domination, seeks to capture the governmental institutions of a nation, in short, seeks to attain control of society, it must first predicate its ambitions and demands upon a solid structure of organized economic power. Demands and move-- ments not so fortified are in the outset doomed to ignominious failure and defeat. This deduction applies particularly to the struggle of the proletariat against the exploiting class.

In our investigation we have clearly defined the seat of the capitalists' economic power, and, therefore, fully appreciate the significance and source of the political and social influence exercised by this class in society. We know that the title of private ownership in the means of production, vested in the capitalist class, is at the bottom of it all. In the face of such a powerful force, what form of economic power can the working class organize with which to be able to overcome and obliterate the property prerogatives of Capitalism?

We are fully aware that all ruling classes in the past have based or established their social supremacy upon some form of ownership, i. e., upon some property prerogative. The patricians of Rome considered birth and the possession of land, cattle and a multitude of slaves a fitting recommendation to rule; the feudal lord pivoted his era of the mailed fist upon the absolute control of the land; and the capitalist is in undisputed possession of the ship of state, by virtue of his absolute control over all the agencies of production in society. The working class, mustering its forces to give battle to the advocates and upholders of the present system, finds itself the only class in the long chain of social development that seeks to acquire the economic and political supremacy in society without possessing or attempting to fortify this supremacy with some property prerogative.

The working class being toolless and stripped of every vestige of property can not organize its economic forces along the lines of ownership. The economic power of the proletariat rests not, as it is and has been the case with all *parasitic* ruling classes, in the power of ownership, but in the power of production: *not in its problematical indispensability as a possessing class, but in its actual indispensability as a producing class.* The physical and intellectual productive faculties of the working class form the groundwork of present day society and symbolize the pulsating blood of our social organism. Consequently, these faculties organized on *a class-conscious* basis and in line with the dictates of economic development; in other words, these physical and intellectual productive forces of the workers organized in the interest of the proletariat represent and form the structure of working class economic power. As can be readily seen, the seat of working class power, different from that of previous ruling classes, does not rest in the usurpation and possession of rights and property respectively, but in the *consciousness of the proletariat's indispensability as a productive agent*—in the consciousness of being the *working* class. *This class-consciousness of the workers is the generator of the economic power of the proletariat.* Recognizing the economic indispensability of the workers in the process of production, and thereby appreciating the role played by the proletariat in the maintenance of society, it is now a simple matter for the class-conscious worker to translate these conceptions into proper forms of organization.

Production being the origin of and maintaining element in social life; production also being solely carried on by the workers; furthermore, exploitation or the appropriation of surplus value also taking place at the point of production; and, again, the point of production being also the seat of the capitalists' economic power, it logically follows that the *class* organization of the workers will first marshal and organize its forces at this point. The organization of the workers along class-conscious lines at the point of production is synonymous to rearing and developing the economic power in the proletariat. Consequently, this power increases as the class-consciousness increases amongst the workers, and their economic and political organizations will grow in the same proportion.

To sum up: The economic power of the worker rests not in some form of ownership or property prerogative, as is the case with the capitalists, but in the recognition of his status as a worker, in the recognition of his economic worth or indispensability— *in his class-consciousness.* In order to assert itself effectively, this class-consciousness must take on certain organized forms on the industrial as well as political field, i. e., must express itself in accord with the requirements of capitalist development in particular and social evolution in general. This phase of the problem will be dealt with in the second part of this article.

II.

IN the first part of this article a detailed examination of the social and economic position or status of the two principal classes in present society was made. This investigation, we believe, has revealed to us clearly the economic functions performed by the different social classes; thereby also exposing the sources or seat of their respective social power. We can at least venture to assert that it has brought home the so important truism that all political or social influence exercised by a social category in a particular historic period is but a reflex of its economic influence or might, i. e., that political power or governmental control does not conquer and cement the industrial supremacy and hegemony for a class, but, on the contrary, that the industrial supremacy of a class is also bound to ultimately insure political power and governmental domination to it. The proper recognition of this fact by the proletariat—a fact which can be amply substantiated by historic and sociological examples—will eventually compel this class to organize and conduct its struggle against Capitalism accordingly. This further implies that the proper appreciation of this fundamental proposition will henceforth actuate the class-conscious workers to concentrate their energies upon the *organization* of their economic power; and this attempt will again animate them to seek to establish the original source of this *potential* force in the working-class.

In our last article we emphasized that the economic power of the workers did not rest in some form of ownership or property prerogative, as is and was the case with all previous ruling classes, but in the recognition of their proletarian status, in the recognition of their economic worth or indispensability —*in their class-consciousness.* From this deduction it follows

that the economic and social influence or power of the proletariat is not, as it has been so often erroneously asserted, to
be found in the form or particular function of an organization,
but in its spirit and theoretical composition. Not the form or
particular functions will affect and determine the principles of
an organization, but the principles will determine the form and
functions. Therefore, it cannot be too emphatically underscored that the power of the proletariat does not in the last
analysis rest in the form or structure, but the spirit of an
organization. Consequently, when certain Socialists attribute
revolutionary vitality and creative power to Industrial Unionism as Industrial Unionism without qualifying it with the word
Socialist, then they commit precisely the same error which
certain pure and simple politicians fall into, when they
seek to "organize the masses into a large political party"
and in their anxiety for success forget and ignore entirely the *Socialist* character of the organization. Primarily,
it is not the question whether the workers are organized
on the economic field along craft or industrial lines, because
we have both forms of organization in existence now
(see Germany and America for classical examples); neither,
whether the workers engage in independent politics, such
politics having been carried on for years by so-called
liberal reform movements and alleged "Socialist" parties;
but whether the economic and political activity is a Socialist
activity; whether the industrial union is a class-conscious union; and whether the Socialist political party is a
truly working-class organization. The yardstick with which
to establish the status of a workers' organization has been
provided in our previous article, and is to be found in the
organization's conception of Capitalism and the consequent
interpretation of the class struggle resulting therefrom. To
a revolutionary Socialist only such an organization is considered class-conscious which affirms unequivocally the inabil-

ity of the workers to improve their economic and social conditions under Capitalism permanently and calls upon the workers to marshal their forces on the economic as well as political field under the banner of not palliation or reform, but revolution. Organizations, therefore, that devote their main efforts to the palliation of effects and the propagation of reforms, even if "ultimately" affirming and "demanding" Socialism, can not be considered class-conscious organizations, and are in reality a greater obstacle to the formation of a genuine proletarian army of the revolution than all the chicanery, economic despotism and social and cultural prerogatives of the capitalist class combined. Class-conscious Socialist action can only be the product of a scientific conception of capitalist production, of a Marxian interpretation of economic and social phenomena, and can, in consequence, have only a certain meaning to the working-class. Therefore it can not mean one thing to one worker and something else to another. It will also be admitted that certain scientific premises and a scientific mode of investigation furnish certain deductions, which again will prescribe or determine a definite mode of action. The mode of action or tactics of a class-conscious movement, as it can be readily gleaned from the preceding, are, therefore, not the fruit of "expediency" or chance, but the product of theoretical clarity and scientific perception. Such being the case, the tactical department of the Socialist movement is, consequently, inseparably connected with the theoretical system of Socialism, being in reality a component part of this system. Therefore, tactical clarity and efficiency in a Socialist movement can only flow from theoretical clarity; a soundness in scientific consciousness and profundity being the father to class-consciousness, and class-consciousness again giving birth to effective class action—the dynamo of class movements.

Having established the original source of working-class

power, and knowing that it rests in the consciousness of the worker appertaining to his economic indispensability, it is now quite a simple proposition to formulate a tactical program for the organization of this industrial might. Before we proceed with this task, it is, however, imperative to re-state in short the objective or the aim of the proletarian struggle. This objective, as emphasized before, is determined first by the Socialist analysis of capitalist production and secondly by the proper appreciation with the aid of Materialistic Conception of History of the historic role allotted to the working-class in the period of evolution. From the application of Historical Materialism and Marxian Economics to social development in general and Capitalism in particular, we are compelled to conclude that the basic cause of the workers' misery and the original source of all class demarcations existing in present society, and the innumerable effects resulting therefrom are to be found in the capitalist or private ownership of the socially produced and operated instruments of wealth production; and that, in consequence, as long as the fundamental antithesis between social production and individual appropriation continues to exist the multifarious other economic and political contradictions would naturally continue to thrive. The immediate and ultimate objective of the Socialist movement must, therefore, concentrate and organize around the demand for the abolition of private ownership in the socially necessary instruments of production (including all land), i. e., must marshal its forces for the shattering of the commodity status in labor-power and the inauguration of the Industrial Republic. Consequently, at this late date of capitalist development, in this period of social turmoil and full-fledged Capitalism, the only demand worthy of unstinted working-class support is the one which demands the unconditional surrender of the capitalist class—the Socialist Commonwealth, nothing less nor more. With this demand as the only immediate and ultimate aim to struggle for, with the social revolution as the objective before it, the Socialist movement can not fail to be a truly revolutionary movement, and must by necessity formulate tactics just as revolutionary as the aim that gave birth to them.

We have seen from the foregoing that the economic power of the workers slumbers in their class-consciousness; furthermore, that this class-consciousness can only be effectively aroused and reared in the proletarians with the aid of *Socialist* education predicated upon a Socialist or revolutionary objective. Therefore, all so-called "Socialist propaganda" and activity not based upon such an aim, or advancing it as the "ultimate demand", and advocating as "immediate demands" an endless string of palliatives or reforms, can not be considered as Socialist activity, and the adherents and votes obtained through such a propaganda can not be considered class-conscious adherents or votes. The Socialist aim must, in consequence, be jealously guarded and kept intact by the Socialist movement and can not be sacrificed to the aspirations of political quacks or charlatans. The question what organic form is this economic power, this proletarian class-consciousness, to take on in its battle against the economic power of the capitalist class is now in order, and will be taken up in as detailed a form as the limited space at our disposal permits.

As an introduction to this phase of Constructive Socialism we desire to affirm the necessity of utilizing both wings, of practising political as well as industrial action in the conduction of the class war. Admitting the imperativeness of both, it now remains to establish the function of each and their relative importance in preparing for and carrying out the act of emancipation.

We will first examine the function played by politics in the class struggle. It is now generally recognized that the existence of a political struggle presupposes the existence of an economic struggle: i. e., that political differences and antagonisms have their origin in economic differences, etc. Therefore, every political struggle is fundamentally an economic struggle; and the eradication of the industrial struggle of the classes spells, consequently, the eradication of politics. The existence of political parties and a political life in general is based upon the existence of classes, which again have their roots in the peculiar property prerogatives inherent in the economic system of a particular historical period. With the disappearance of economic classes social and political classes will also disappear. Therefore, as stated before, the abolition of all property prerogatives in economic life by the Socialist workers also implies the abolition of all political differences and the automatic ceasing of the political struggle. The political struggle, as carried on by the class-conscious workers and pursuing but one objective, can, therefore, be utilized and exploited by the proletariat for only one purpose, namely to abolish Capitalism. By using the political arm in this manner, the political victory of the workers will naturally be synonymous with the abolition of politics—the abolition of classes. Thus the political struggle is engaged in by the workers to carry on revolutionary Socialist propaganda. This struggle has, however, purely a destructive function, because a general political victory of Socialism spells the downfall of political government and the advent of the Industrial Republic, a society without classes and political antagonisms. The possibility of such a decisive Socialist victory, however, presupposes the existence of certain industrial organizations of the proletariat necessary, first, to impart power to the political demand and, second, to *perform the act of socialization.* And this leads us to the function played by industrial action in the class struggle.

We know that the economic power of the workers rests in the consciousness of their economic indispensability as productive agents. To organize this economic indispensability at the point of production *along class-conscious lines and in accord with the dictates of modern economic evolution* is, as already stated before, therefore, an urgent requirement of the hour and on par with generating and accumulating proletarian economic vitality. Class-conscious Socialist organization at the point of production, that is in the industries, however, is essential for a twofold reason and must be accomplished in a definite way.

In the first place such an organization or Socialist Industrial Union is an organized expression of proletarian class-consciousness in a certain industry. This organized expression announces to society that the productive facilities of this particular industry are not only socially operated, but also in the control of Socialist workers, who are only waiting for the signal to supplement social production with social ownership. Of course the form of such an organization must also be in accord with the requirements of economic evolution; and being the product *of class-conscious workers* is bound to be in line with a scientific conception of capitalist production. Such a conception clearly shows the insufficiency and antiquatedness of the craft form of unionism, a form absolutely out of joint with the highly centralized character of capitalist industry. The Historical Materialist, and every scientific Socialist is a Historical Materialist, constructs and adapts his organization to meet the demands of social requirements. He studies economic and social conditions with a view of employing the knowledge gained therefrom to improve the position of the working-class in its fight for emancipation. Therefore, when the Historical Materialist emphasizes the necessity of organizing the workers along the lines of Socialist Industrial Unionism his plea is pivoted upon certain sound perceptions. The reason for the class character of every form of proletarian organization has been sufficiently underscored and need not be dwelled upon any more. What must now be shown is the necessity for this particular form of unionism: the necessity for Industrial Unionism.

Industrial Unionism, like all previous forms of economic organization which preceded it, is but a product of the particular character of the industries from which it emanated. The complex and centralized form of production, which gave birth to Industrial Unionism, can again on the one hand be attributed to the concentration of wealth into ever fewer hands, and on the other to an ever increasing social character of the machines or instruments of production. The competitive struggle with its process of elimination, and the discoveries and inventions on the field of mechanical and economic evolution are responsible for the highly corporate and at times monopolistic character of industries, and have given the death blow to small production and also every form of craft organization bound up therewith. Industrial Unionism is, therefore, but a reflex of industrialized (understand highly centralized) capitalist production, and as such only an obedient servant of economic evolution. Therefore, to expect proletarian class-consciousness to assume any other form of organic expression on the industrial field than that of Industrial Unionism would be to expect the impossible to be possible, or the sharp observers to be blind.

The Socialist Industrial Union, as the organized expression of proletarian economic indispensability on the industrial field, fulfills two functions in the present struggle. Aside fom waging the every-day struggle of the workers against exploitation, a struggle that is waged distinctly with the view of abolishing exploitation, and which is, similar to the Socialist political struggle, purely destructive, the Socialist Industrial Union also performs a constructive function of great importance. This constructive function consists in organizing the productive faculties of the workers not only in line with the requirements of highly socialized capitalist production, but also in line with the requirements of Socialist production in the making. It is an axiom of Historical Materialism that the shell of every new society develops within the womb of the old. We also know that the social elements in capitalist production symbolize the formative stages of a new economic order. However, a class-conscious organization along the lines of highly centralized social production, and truly manifesting the economic power of the workers, does more than give social expression to these formative stages—it really symbolizes the future structure of the Industrial Republic in the process of formation. Therefore, in the same proportion as the Socialist Industrial Union movement develops, in just that degree does the economic and political power of the capitalist class diminish, and the economic and political power of the workers increase. The growth of the Socialist Industrial Union Movement signifies the ever quicker approaching destruction of capitalist production on the one hand, and the ever more efficient organization of Socialist production on the other. Upon the economic power vested within the Socialist Industrial Union, historical evolution has, consequently, conferred two duties: the first, to stand as the organized economic might behind the revolutionary objective of the proletariat—to serve as the buckler and sword of the social revolution; the second, to insure and organize the fruits of the revolution—to take and hold the industries in the interest of the Industrial Republic. In the first capacity, it serves as the agent and executor of the Socialist political party, and in the second it functions as the organized productive administration of the Industrial Republic.

In concluding we wish again to emphasize that the economic and social might of the proletariat does not rest in a certain *form of economic organization,* as for instance Industrial Unionism; furthermore, that the structural or organic phases can never impart power to an organization; but that this economic might is lodged in the class-consciousness of the workers; however, that this class-consciousness can only be derived from a Socialist conception of Capitalism, which again imparts to the workers the Constructive Elements of Socialism, clearly outlining the functions of revolutionary Socialist political action and Socialist Industrial Unionism. In consequence, a worker can be an Industrial

Unionist without being a Socialist, but not a Socialist without being an Industrial Unionist. Industrial Unionism to be effective and to have the historic significance accorded to it above must, therefore, be squarely planted upon Socialist principles and be vitalized by the dynamic forces of class-consciousness.

The advocacy of uncompromising Socialist principles is, in consequence, a fundamental demand for all Socialist agitation. Such Socialist propaganda can revolve around only one demand —Socialism, fighting and repudiating all other agitation and principles as reactionary or capitalistic.

Advertisements of Books on Socialism and kindred subjects

Radical Review's Book Department

202 EAST 17th STREET

Tel., Stuyvesant 1446   NEW YORK CITY

Ancient Lowly—Osborn Ward, 2 Vol. ....@ $2.00
Ancient Society—L. H. Morgan 1.50
Capital—Karl Marx ....@ 2.00
Critique of Political Economy—Karl Marx 1.00
Wage, Labor and Capital and Discourse on Free Trade—
    Karl Marx .... .50
Value, Price and Profit—Karl Marx .... .50
The Communist Manifesto with Liebknecht's "No Com-
    promise" .... .50
The Paris Commune—Karl Marx .... .50
Revolution and Counter-Revolution, or Germany in 1848
    —Karl Marx .... .50
The Eighteenth Brumaire—Karl Marx .... .50
Philosophical Essays—Jos. Dietzgen 1.00
Positive Outcome of Philosophy—Jos. Dietzgen 1.00
Feuerbach, Roots of Socialist Philosophy—Fred. Engels .50
Origin of the Family—Frederick Engels .... .50
Landmarks of Scientific Socialism—Fred. Engels 1.00
Socialism, Utopian and Scientific—Frederick Engels .. .50
Essays on the Materialist Conception of History—
    Labriola 1.00
The Class Struggle—Karl Kautsky .... .50
Ethics and the Materialistic Conception of History—
    Karl Kautsky .... .50
Evolution of Property—Paul Lafargue .... .50
Woman under Socialism—August Bebel 1.00
High Cost of Living—Karl Kautsky .... .50
High Cost of Living—Arnold Petersen .... .15
Vulgar Economy—Daniel De Leon .... .15
Marx on Mallock; or Facts vs. Fiction—Daniel De Leon .05
Fifteen Questions—Daniel De Leon .... .20
Flashlights of the Amsterdam Congress—Daniel De
    Leon .... .15
Two Pages from Roman History—Daniel De Leon .... .15
Berger's Hits and Misses—Daniel De Leon .... .15
Industrial Unionism—Debs and De Leon .... .10

Add 10 cents per volume for postage.

Reform or Revolution

or

Socialism and Socialist Politics

By

KARL DANNENBERG

A work presenting a thorough examination of Opportunism; lucidly exposing the unscientific position and popular fallacis of so-called Socialist reform movements: A Marxian indictment of Revisionism in action

---

Price, 10 Cents (*12 Cents postpaid*)

Special Rates to Dealers and Organizations

The Radical Review Publishing Association

202 East 17th Street, New York City

The Co-Operative Press

119

15 Spruce St., New York